FRIENDS INDEED

FRIENDS INDEED

THE SPECIAL RELATIONSHIP OF ISRAEL AND THE UNITED STATES

NORMAN H. FINKELSTEIN

The Millbrook Press
Brookfield, Connecticut

Grateful acknowledgment is made to the following for the use of copyrighted material: Little, Brown and Company for *Years of Upheaval* by Henry Kissinger, copyright 1982 by Henry Kissinger; Penguin USA for quotations from *Talking Peace* by Jimmy Carter, copyright 1993 by Jimmy Carter; The Putnam Publishing Group for quotations from *My Life* by Golda Meir, copyright 1975 by Golda Meir

Library of Congress Cataloging-in-Publication Data
Finkelstein, Norman H.
Friends indeed : the special relationship of Israel and the United States / Norman H. Finkelstein.
p.   cm.
Includes bibliographical references and index.
Summary: Explores United States–Israel relations since the founding of Israel in 1948 within the context of ongoing strife and attempts at peace in the Middle East, the political climate in the U.S., and the opinions of the Jewish community.
ISBN 0-7613-0114-3 (lib. bdg.)
1. United States—Foreign relations—Israel—Juvenile literature. 2. Israel—Foreign relations—United States—Juvenile literature. 3. United States—Foreign relations—1945–1989—Juvenile literature. 4. United States—Foreign relations—1989– —Juvenile literature. [1. United States—Foreign relations—Israel. 2. Israel—Foreign relations—United States.] I. Title.
E183.8.I7F575   1998
327.7305694—dc21   97-28108   CIP   AC

Photographs courtesy of: Embassy of Israel: pp. 18, 79, 93, 145; Underwood & Underwood/Corbis-Bettmann: p. 21; Corbis-Bettmann: p. 24; Harry S. Truman Library: pp. 37 (#59-1015), 44 (#68-1886), 54 (#59-1584-1); John F. Kennedy Library: pp. 51 (#PX 66-5), 72 (#ST 212-52-61); UPI/Corbis-Bettmann: p. 59; National Archives: p. 89; Gerald R. Ford Library: pp. 104 (#A9309-2), 108 (#A6282-13A); Jimmy Carter Library: pp. 120 (#C7421-18/18A), 123 (#C10030-13); Reuters/Corbis-Bettmann: p. 138; Agence France Presse/Corbis-Bettmann: p. 149

Published by The Millbrook Press, Inc.
2 Old New Milford Road, Brookfield, Connecticut 06804

16.90

CONTENTS

ACKNOWLEDGMENTS

I wish to acknowledge the dedicated librarians and archivists who assisted me in researching this book. I am especially indebted to Geir Gundersen and Nancy Mirshah at the Gerald R. Ford Library in Ann Arbor, Michigan; Alan Goodrich at the John F. Kennedy Library in Boston, Massachusetts; and Dr. Maurice Tuchman at the Hebrew College Library, Brookline, Massachusetts.

I am especially indebted to the Gerald R. Ford Foundation for a study grant, which permitted my research in the collections at the Ford Library.

I also wish to thank Sally Kepnes at the Government of Israel Economic Office in Boston and Barukh Binah, Minister-Counselor for Public Affairs at the Embassy of Israel in Washington, D.C., for their assistance in locating relevant background material.

Finally, I thank my wife, Rosalind, for her unending patience and understanding.

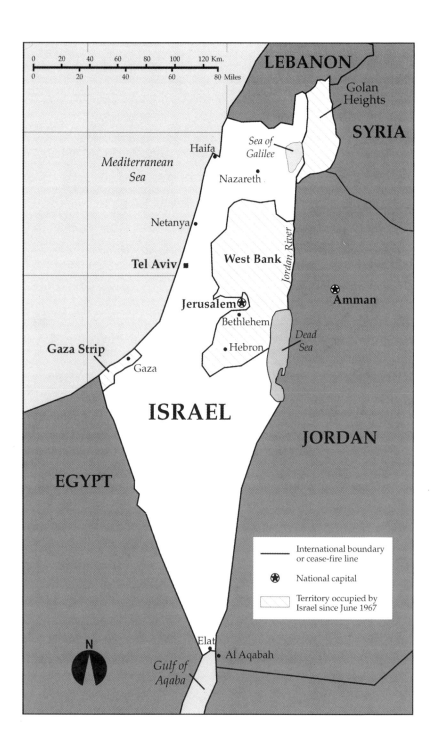

LEBANON

Golan
Heights

SYRIA

Mediterranean
Sea

Haifa

Sea of
Galilee

Nazareth

Netanya

Jordan River

Tel Aviv

West Bank

Jerusalem

Amman

Bethlehem

Dead
Sea

Gaza Strip

Hebron

Gaza

ISRAEL

JORDAN

EGYPT

International boundary
or cease-fire line

National capital

Territory occupied by
Israel since June 1967

N

Elat

Al Aqabah

Gulf of
Aqaba

0   20   40   60   80   100   120 Km.
0   20   40   60   80 Miles

INTRODUCTION

The United States was born in 1776; the State of Israel in 1948. Although the United States is nearly four times older than the nation of Israel, the history of the Jewish homeland began thousands of years earlier. Since the beginning in the days of the Bible, there has been an unbroken connection of the Jewish people to the land they call Eretz Yisroel—the Land of Israel. This small piece of earth has an importance to Jews that is not only historical and emotional but also religious.

At its heart is God's agreement with Abraham to "establish my covenant as an everlasting covenant between me and you and your descendants after you. . . . The whole land of Canaan, where you are now an alien, I will give as an everlasting possession to you and your descendants after you; and I will be their God." (Genesis 17:7-8)

Even when physically separated from that land for short or long periods, Jews never allowed themselves to forget their homeland. Each Passover, no matter where they live, Jews conclude their Seder meals with these heartfelt words: "Next year in Jerusalem!"

We learn from history about many peoples who were conquered by stronger neighbors and then disappeared from the face of the earth. But unlike the Edomites, Sumerians, and Phoenicians, the Jews survived. Each new threat to survival strengthened the Jews' attachment to their religion, culture, and land.

In 586 B.C., the mighty Babylonian army sacked the city of Jerusalem and reduced the Holy Temple of the Jewish people to ashes. The political, religious, and educational leaders of Jewish society were forced from their country and taken as captives to Babylon. They consoled themselves with the hope that their exile would soon be over. Forty-five years passed before they were allowed to return. By that time most Jews had accommodated themselves to the stylish and comfortable life outside the Holy Land, and only a small, dedicated group undertook the difficult journey back and rebuilt the Temple. The rest established a Jewish life for themselves in Babylon while retaining close ties with their homeland. Their pattern was followed by later generations of Jews, including those who settled in Europe and the United States.

In A.D. 70 the city of Jerusalem was captured by the Romans. For the second time in Jewish history, the Temple, Judaism's central focus and authority, was destroyed; this time it would not be rebuilt. Most of the Jews were banished from their own land and began a new and long chapter in their history. Their two-thousand-year exile from Palestine—the Diaspora, Greek for dispersion—scattered the Jewish people to the four corners of the earth. Unlike the first exile, which lasted less than fifty years, this one lasted nearly two thousand, until 1948.

Building upon the lessons of the first exile in Babylon, the Jews adapted their religion by substituting prayer and study for Holy Temple ritual. Rabbinic Judaism and the synagogue became the foundations of Jewish life. These two innovations allowed Jews, no matter where they lived, to continue their religious practices without Palestine and the

Temple. But wherever they went, unable to return to their homeland now ruled by others, Jews did not forget Jerusalem in their hearts and prayers.

Within a few centuries there were established Jewish communities throughout the Arab world and Europe. Jewish belief in monotheism—one God—gave rise to other major religions: first, Christianity and later, Islam. As Christianity grew to become the national religion of the Roman Empire, the lives of the Jews of Europe became increasingly difficult. Jews were accused of having killed Jesus. They were subject to religious intolerance, persecution, and discrimination. As the major non-Christian group in Europe, they were looked upon with suspicion and hatred wherever they settled. Over the years Jews were expelled from one European country after another, while others were restricted to specific areas called ghettos.

Beginning with the French Revolution in 1789, a wave of freedom and enlightenment descended upon the people of Europe. For Jews this was an impossible dream come true. The confining spirit of the ghetto was broken and Jews could, for the first time, dream of attaining rights of citizenship in the countries where they had lived for so long. Jews in Western Europe could enter professions that were previously closed to them. They could attend public schools and gain admission to universities. Of perhaps greater importance was their right to equal justice, to political activity, and even to serve in their country's army.

The spirit of enlightenment also affected traditional Jewish religious life. Moses Mendelssohn, the eighteenth-century German Jewish philosopher, set the stage for the later birth of Reform and Conservative Judaism when he advised his fellow Jews to "adopt the mores and constitution of the country in which you find yourself, but be steadfast in upholding the religion of your fathers, too. Bear both burdens as well as you can."

That breath of fresh air did not yet mean total equality. It was difficult to erase centuries of superstition and hatred with the stroke of a pen, and in spite of certain freedoms, anti-Semitism (hatred of Jews) still flourished. Life for Jews in Russia and Eastern Europe remained particularly harsh.

Although there had always been a Jewish presence in the Holy Land, some nineteenth-century European Jews began to work for the reestablishment of a Jewish state in Palestine as a way to solve the problems of anti-Semitism. This movement, called Zionism, was led by Theodor Herzl (1860–1904), a noted Austrian journalist. The First Zionist Congress in 1897 established the political and organizational groundwork, which led to the founding of the modern State of Israel.

Centuries of European anti-Semitism resulted in the Holocaust. By the time World War II ended in 1945, six million Jewish men, women, and children, one half of the Jews of Europe, were dead. As survivors staggered out of the concentration camps, the world agreed with the Zionists that the time had finally come for the reestablishment of a Jewish state.

The 1948 *Declaration* proclaiming Israel's birth states in part:

> The Land of Israel was the birthplace of the Jewish people. Here their spiritual, religious and political identity was shaped. Here they first attained to statehood, created cultural values of national and universal significance and gave to the world the eternal Book of Books.

> After being forcibly exiled from their land, the people kept faith with it throughout their dispersion and never ceased to pray and hope for their return to it and for the restoration in it of their political freedom.

FROM DREAM
TO REALITY

*Zionism is the pilgrim inspiration and impulse over
again: The descendants of the Pilgrim Fathers should
not find it hard to understand and sympathize with it.*

—Louis D. Brandeis

Israel has never been far removed from the mind of America.
From 1620 onward, Americans have held a special fasci-
nation with Jewish biblical heroes and the ancient Jewish
homeland, known at various times as the Holy Land, Zion,
Palestine, or Israel. The Pilgrims who arrived on board the
Mayflower strongly identified with the people of the Old
Testament and compared their new home with biblical
Canaan. Pilgrim children bore biblical names. During
America's colonial period, study of the Hebrew language
was required at Harvard, Yale, and King's College (later
known as Columbia University). After the Revolutionary
War, Benjamin Franklin proposed that the Great Seal of
the new and independent United States depict the biblical
story of Moses crossing the Red Sea. While that scene was
not chosen, the Liberty Bell was inscribed with words from
Leviticus: "Proclaim liberty to all the inhabitants thereof."

While Jewish values and heritage were idealized in the early years of the United States, individual Jews were often viewed differently. The Jews who came to America had experienced rampant discrimination in Europe; so in the New World they kept a wary eye open. Religious differences sometimes made Jews feel unwelcome, and in certain colonies specific laws restricted the rights of non-Christians. "No person who does not profess the Christian religion can be admitted free of this colony."

With the end of the Revolutionary War, Jews and other minorities gained acceptance when Article VI of the United States Constitution guaranteed that "no religious test shall ever be required as a qualification to any office or public trust under the United States." In a 1790 letter to the Jewish community of Newport, Rhode Island, George Washington wrote: "For happily the Government of the United States, which gives to bigotry no sanction, to persecution no assistance, requires only that they who live under its protection, should demean themselves as good citizens. . . ."

In spite of federal guarantees, some states maintained discriminatory rules against Jews well into the nineteenth century. Jewish residents of Maryland, for example, could not hold state office since they could not declare "belief in the Christian religion." In 1818, Thomas Kennedy, a Christian member of the Maryland legislature, filed a bill "to extend to the sect of people professing the Jewish religion, the same rights and privileges that are enjoyed by Christians."

"There are not Jews in the county from whence I came nor have I the slightest acquaintance with any Jew in the world," Kennedy said. He simply believed that religion was "a question which rests, or ought to rest, between man and his creator alone." The "Jew Bill" was defeated year after year until it was finally passed in 1824.

In 1820, Mordecai Manuel Noah, a well-known Jewish political figure, petitioned the New York legislature for permission to establish a settlement on Grand Island in the Niagara River near Buffalo. His goal was a "city of refuge . . . [for persecuted European Jews] where they can enjoy that peace, comfort and happiness, which have been denied them through the intolerance and misgovernment of former ages." Noah enjoyed support from many influential non-Jews. Even before the idea of a Grand Island refuge, President John Adams told Noah in 1818, "I really wish the Jews again in Judea, an independent nation. . . ."

In September 1825, amid military pomp and ceremony, Ararat, Noah's "asylum for the Jews," was formally established on Grand Island as a "temporary and provisionary refuge." The noble cause eventually failed but not Noah's belief in the need for a Jewish homeland. Later in life, realizing there could be only one site for a Jewish land, Noah wrote a newspaper article urging readers to support Jews "by helping to restore them to the land of their forefathers and the possession of their ancient heritage."

By 1830 there were approximately 15,000 Jews in the United States. Many were descendants of Jews expelled from Spain in 1492. Forced to flee religious persecution in Portuguese Brazil, a small band of 23 Jewish men, women, and children reached New Amsterdam in 1654 and formed the first Jewish settlement in North America. In spite of early difficulties, they quickly established a foothold in the young country.

Beginning in 1848, a major wave of immigration brought a large number of Jews from Germany to the United States, many of them with liberal religious views. Speaking at Charleston, South Carolina, in 1841, at the establishment of the first Reform temple in the United States, a rabbi said, "This country is our Palestine, this city our Jerusalem, this house of God our Temple."

Since the destruction of the Second Temple in Jerusalem by the Romans in the year 70, Jews had been driven out of their own land. Their two-thousand-year exile scattered the Jewish people all over the world. No matter where they settled, religious intolerance usually forced them to move elsewhere. After Emperor Constantine declared Christianity to be the national religion of the Roman Empire, the effects upon the Jews of Europe became increasingly unbearable. Jews were looked upon with suspicion wherever they settled. Religious discrimination forced the Jews to become a people apart, living on European soil but not considered equal to their non-Jewish neighbors.

The period of freedom and enlightenment that came to the people of Western Europe with the French Revolution of 1789 did not erase discrimination against Jews. While Jews in France, Britain, and Germany benefited from their new rights, Jews in Russia continued to suffer.

Under the rule of the czars, anti-Semitism had been an instrument of government policy. "Pogrom," the term for planned violence against Jews and their property, is of Russian origin. After a particularly devastating series of attacks against Jews in the early 1880s, Russian Jews responded in several ways. A large number saw the hopelessness of their situation and emigrated. By the outbreak of World War I in 1914, millions had crossed the Atlantic to begin new lives in the United States. Others became involved in the activities of Jewish organizations such as "Hovevey Zion," or Lovers of Zion, which promoted a return to Palestine, the ancient Jewish homeland. Even during their worst suffering throughout the centuries, Jews always yearned for a return to their Holy Land.

The immediate goals of the Zionists were to develop organized Jewish immigration to Palestine and revive Hebrew language and culture. For centuries classical Hebrew had been reserved exclusively for prayer and religious study. Yiddish, based on medieval German, had became the everyday language of European Jews.

Outside the closely knit Zionist community, few paid attention to the utopian hope of reestablishing the Jewish homeland after a two-thousand-year exile. The publication of a little book in 1896 by Dr. Theodor Herzl revolutionized the Jewish world. This book, *The Jewish State*, was a call to action. In it, Herzl laid out a blueprint for solving the problems Jews had faced for centuries. The Jews, Herzl wrote, no matter how assimilated or patriotic, were viewed as strangers. The legal rights they may have gained could not erase the centuries-old traditions of anti-Semitism. The solution? A country of their own. "We are a people," he wrote, "one people." There was no doubt in his mind about the correctness of his idea and its ultimate success. "The Jews who wish for a State shall have it, and they deserve to have it," he declared.

Herzl may have been a dreamer, but he was not naive. He knew that the establishment of a Jewish state required the assent and cooperation of the world's most powerful nations. Without this international political support, there could be no success. No new nation could long survive without international acceptance. Also the Jews themselves had to organize and lobby for the right to their own land. Herzl quickly found himself the acclaimed leader of the Zionist cause. He succeeded where other Zionists had not precisely because, unlike them, he was a westernized, assimilated Jew with easy access to the offices of world leaders. He had taken the problem of anti-Semitism beyond the narrow confines of the Zionist world and made its solution dependent as much on international diplomacy as on Jewish self-determination.

Herzl knew that he needed to create a central structure to organize the Zionist movement. To that end he proposed a congress of Zionists from around the world. For the first time in nearly two thousand years there would be a Jewish national assembly to deliberate on the future of the Jewish people. Finally, Jews would be able to take control of their destiny as a people by creating a vibrant Jewish spirit. The chain of persecution and discrimination would be broken

Although Theodor Herzl was not the first to suggest the need for a Jewish homeland, he was the first to gain a widespread audience for Zionism. His ideas, published in a book called The Jewish State, *included the practical need for international recognition of such a homeland.*

by a new political force capable of leading the Jews to action. The First Zionist Congress opened in Basel, Switzerland, on August 27, 1897. "We are here to lay the foundation stone of the house which is to shelter the Jewish nation," Herzl told the excited delegates.

"The Basel Program" adopted by the Congress stated the goal of the Zionist movement as the establishment of a home for the Jewish people in Palestine secured by international law and recognition. To that end, Herzl embarked on a diplomatic offensive targeted mainly at Turkey, which then ruled Palestine. "At Basel I founded the Jewish State," Herzl later wrote in his diary. "If I said this out loud today, I would be answered by universal laughter. Perhaps in five years, and certainly in fifty, everyone will know it."[1]

Of all the delegates to the first Congress, just one was American. Small Zionist organizations had been founded in America by Russian Jewish immigrants who arrived after 1881 but did not attract much attention. Although most immigrant Jews were supportive, they were too busy becoming "real Americans" to join organizations.

A year later, three delegates represented the small American Zionist community. One, a young Reform rabbi by the name of Stephen S. Wise, felt as if he had "suffered a rebirth." He later wrote: "I was a Jew by faith up to the day of the Congress . . . [but] at Basel . . . the Jewish people became my own."[2] Wise seemingly was the unlikeliest person to champion the Zionist cause. He was an "uptowner," a Reform rabbi and the son of German immigrants. In New York, successful descendants of German Jewish immigrants tended to be Reform Jews and live in the well-to-do uptown sections of Manhattan. The recent Eastern European Jewish immigrants crowded into the downtown Lower East Side. While the Reform movement in Judaism was nearly unanimous in its opposition to Zionism, the "downtowners," Jewish immigrants from Russia, were in favor. These Yiddish-speaking arrivals strongly felt the need for a Jewish homeland. The Union of American Hebrew Congregations, composed mainly of German Jews deeply assimilated into American life, declared in an 1898 statement: "We are unalterably opposed to political Zionism. The Jews are not a nation but a religious Community. . . . America is our Zion." Indeed, Stephen Wise did not fit the description of the "typical" Zionist.

Upon his return from Basel, Stephen Wise helped organize a Zionist convention in New York to combine independent groups into the Federation of American Zionists (FAZ), which later became the Zionist Organization of America (ZOA). Most of the members were Yiddish-speaking Russian immigrants. Wise traveled frequently to speak on behalf of Zionism and raise money for the cause. In a speech at New York's Cooper Union in 1900, he told those present to be proud of Zionism. "Say that you are an American Jew and strive for the best principles of the race, and you will be respected and the Zionist name honored."[3]

Continuing a tradition of Christian support for the establishment of a Jewish homeland, the Reverend William E. Blackstone, a noted Chicago clergyman, had circulated in 1891 a petition supporting a Jewish state in Palestine as "an inalienable possession." The petition, signed by more than four hundred notable Americans, both Jewish and non-Jewish, was presented to President Benjamin Harrison. In *Innocents Abroad*, a firsthand account of his trip to Palestine, Mark Twain wrote of "the long prophesied assembly of the Jews in Palestine from the four quarters of the world, and the restoration of their ancient power and grandeur."

In 1903 the world was shocked by brutal events in the little Russian town of Kishinev. In a particularly well-planned and savage pogrom directed by Russian government officials, nearly fifty Jews were killed and thousands more savagely attacked. In the United States a petition denouncing the massacre was signed by many members of Congress and forwarded to the Russian government by

Rabbi Stephen S. Wise (left) was an important figure in the early Zionist movement in the United States. Even as he was founding the American Jewish Congress and organizing massive demonstrations in support of the movement, he was aiding his country in World War I by working as a laborer in a shipbuilding yard. Here he is pictured with his eighteen-year-old son.

President Theodore Roosevelt. The Russians were genuinely surprised by the world reaction.

In response to the violence against Jews in Russia, a number of prominent "uptown" Jewish Americans, including Louis Marshall, a noted lawyer; Jacob Schiff, a financier; Cyrus Sulzberger, publisher of *The New York Times*; and Julius Rosenwald, the president of Sears, Roebuck and Company, formed the American Jewish Committee (AJC) in 1906. The Committee was the country's first civil-rights organization formed to "take concerted action against the constant and ever increasing efforts to traduce the good name of the Jew." Although initially dedicated to safeguarding the rights of Russian Jews, its work soon broadened to improve the legal and social conditions of all Jews and other Americans.

In spite of the freedoms that Jews experienced in America, the specter of anti-Semitism was never far behind. In 1915, Leo Frank, the Jewish manager of an Atlanta, Georgia, pencil factory, was found guilty of murdering a teenage girl and sentenced to death. The governor of Georgia doubted the evidence of the hate-filled trial and commuted the sentence to life imprisonment. Nonetheless, Frank was dragged from a jail cell and lynched by an angry mob. In spite of the many benefits America offered, the killing of Leo Frank "convinced many Jews of their vulnerability in the United States."

Concerned primarily with civil rights, the American Jewish Committee had not added Zionism to its agenda. Indeed, Zionism might have remained an insignificant aspect of American Jewish life had it not been for one person. Louis D. Brandeis was a famous Boston lawyer. Born in 1856, the son of Jewish immigrants, he grew up in Louisville, Kentucky, "free from Jewish contacts or traditions." In a 1910 interview with Boston's *Jewish Advocate* newspaper, he expressed sympathy "with those Jews who are working for the revival of a Jewish state in Palestine." His embrace of Zionism immediately thrust him to the fore-front of the tiny movement.

He approached his Zionist work with zeal. "Organize, organize, organize, until every Jewish American must stand up and be counted with us. . ." he said. He traveled the country speaking in support of the cause. To immigrant Jews in Chelsea, Massachusetts, he said, "We should all support the Zionist movement whether you or I are interested or never think of going to Palestine." To Reform rabbis concerned that support of Zionism was unpatriotic, he said, "Let no American imagine that Zionism is inconsistent with Patriotism. Every American Jew who aids in advancing the Jewish settlement in Palestine, though he feels that neither he nor his descendants will ever live there, will likewise be a better man and a better American for doing so. . . . Loyalty to America demands . . . that each American Jew become a Zionist."[4]

Judge Julian W. Mack was one of the few American Jewish Committee officers who was also an active Zionist. The AJC had become the most important of the national Jewish organizations. Its officers and members were wealthy and politically influential. They were concerned that the question of "dual loyalty" would raise questions about their Americanism. "I never had the slightest fear," Judge Mack said, "that any of those ideas will make the Jews of this country any less good Americans. . . . There is no difference in my mind between the nationality of the Jews of this country and the nationality of the Germans and the Irish of this country. . . ." He echoed the same thoughts as Brandeis, who said, "To be good Americans, we must be better Jews, and to be better Jews, we must become Zionists."

In 1916, Louis D. Brandeis was nominated to the U.S. Supreme Court by his friend President Woodrow Wilson. Wilson "did not see any contradiction between a special humanitarian interest in the Jews of Palestine and American interests." Wilson also believed in the right of all people

*Zionism had its strong advocates, but it was
Supreme Court Justice Louis Brandeis who brought
it to the attention of the American Jewish Committee.
The considerable strength and influence of both
Brandeis and the Committee helped to make
Zionism an issue in the U.S. government.*

to determine their own national futures. The son of a Protestant minister, Wilson was also strongly attracted to the Zionist cause on religious grounds.

Just prior to the outbreak of World War I in 1914, an emergency meeting of American Zionists elected Brandeis president of the Provisional Executive Committee. In his acceptance speech, Brandeis said, "I find Jews possessed of those qualities which we of the twentieth century seek to develop in our struggle for justice and democracy." At the beginning of the war, there were less than 20,000 Zionist members among the 2.5 million Jews in America. By the end of the war that number had jumped to 125,000.

Zionist hopes worldwide were raised during the war by the Balfour Declaration of 1917. Lord Balfour, the British foreign minister, supported the establishment of a Jewish national homeland. Britain also wanted to influence American public opinion in favor of entering the war on Britain's side against Germany.

The words of the Balfour Declaration were carefully crafted. "His Majesty's Government view with favor the establishment in Palestine of a national home for the Jewish people and will use their best endeavors to facilitate the achievement of this object, it being clearly understood that nothing shall be done which may prejudice the religious rights of existing non-Jewish communities in Palestine or the rights and political status enjoyed by Jews in any other country."

Although the Balfour Declaration was couched in language that satisfied Jews while trying not to alarm the Arabs who occupied Palestine, it represented a major success to Zionists. For the first time, a major international power had officially recognized the right of the Jewish people to reestablish its homeland in Palestine. Jews in New York celebrated with a huge parade, the first Jewish parade in the city. Brandeis and other American Zionists petitioned American leaders to endorse the Balfour Declaration. Secretary of State Robert Lansing, anxious not to deviate from American neutrality in the war, which it maintained until it joined the Allied Forces in 1917, wrote to President Wilson: ". . . We should go slowly in announcing a policy . . . we are not at war with Turkey and therefore should avoid any appearance of favoring taking territory from that Empire by force . . . [also] many Christian sects . . . would resent turning the Holy Land over to [Jews]."

One Reform Jewish leader, opposed to Zionism, wrote President Wilson, "Please do not take America from me . . . my flag is Red, White and Blue, how then can I have any other national homeland?"[5] Among American Jews, that view was in the minority. Even while the American Jewish Committee issued a statement against the establishment of a Jewish state, they still endorsed the Balfour Declaration and expressed sympathy "with the efforts of Zionists which aim to secure for Jews at present living in lands of oppression a refuge in Palestine or elsewhere. . . ." John Haynes Holmes, a Protestant minister and close friend of Rabbi Stephen Wise, was a supporter of Zionism. "Zionism has given to American Jews a vision," he wrote. "It has given to American Jews, as to all Jews, a solution of their age-old problem."

Justice Brandeis and Rabbi Wise spent the summer of 1918 convincing President Wilson to support the Balfour Declaration. Finally, on August 31, in advance of Rosh Hashanah, the Jewish New Year holiday, President Wilson sent a letter to Rabbi Wise. ". . . I welcome the opportunity," wrote the president, "to express the satisfaction I have felt in the progress of the Zionist movement in the United States and the Allied countries since the declaration of Mr. Balfour on behalf of the British Government, of Great Britain's approval of the establishment in Palestine of a national home for the Jewish people."[6]

In 1918, Rabbi Wise founded the American Jewish Congress to counteract the perceived elitism of the older American Jewish Committee. Wise envisioned an organization that would attract a broad representation of American Jews. At the conclusion of World War I, all interested parties prepared for a peace conference in Paris consisting of the Allied victors. The Congress sent Wise and a delegation to Paris. Its mission was to convince the peace conference to "recognize the aspirations and historic claims of the Jewish people with regard to Palestine. . . ." The delegation went with the blessing of President Wilson, who, before their departure, assured them that "in Palestine there shall be laid the foundation of Jewish commonwealth."[7] Indeed, the peace treaty with Turkey included the text of the Balfour Declaration. Because it had allied itself with Germany, Turkey lost control of Palestine, which was turned over to Great Britain as a territorial mandate of the League of Nations, which was formed after the war.

During the 1920s the Zionist movement in the United States was torn by internal debate. Assimilated Jewish leaders such as Brandeis and Wise competed with the Yiddish-speaking Eastern European immigrants allied with respected scientist Dr. Chaim Weizmann, successor to Theodor Herzl as head of the World Zionist Organization. In 1921, Weizmann visited the United States. In a grueling fund-raising tour of major American cities, he stirred audiences to action. He understood that American Jews were not about to move to Palestine, so he focused instead on the importance of a Jewish state for all Jews. "If you want your position to be secure elsewhere," he said repeatedly, "you must have a portion of Jewry which is at home, in its own country."

American Jews continued to raise money for the Zionist cause and, despite internal dissension, began to realize the potential of focused political power. In 1922 both houses of Congress passed a joint resolution signed by President Warren G. Harding stating that ". . . the United States of America favors the establishment in Palestine of a national home for the Jewish people. . . ."

Since the early 1880s successive waves of immigration had increased the Jewish population of Palestine. These waves were called *Aliyot* (singular: *Aliya*), from the Hebrew word meaning "going up." The First Aliya, from 1881 to 1903, brought 25,000 idealistic young Russian "Lovers of Zion" to Palestine fleeing pogroms. This was the period in which nearly two million other Jews immigrated to the United States. The Second Aliya of 40,000 Jews, from 1903 to 1914, was instigated by the Russians' massacre of Jews in Kishinev. The Third Aliya, from 1919 to 1923, resulted from the excesses of the Russian Revolution of 1917 and brought 35,000 more Jews to Palestine. The Fourth Aliya, from 1924 to 1928, brought 67,000 mainly middle-class, urban Jews from Poland. Many of these energetic Polish Jews moved to Palestine because in 1924 the United States had imposed harsh restrictions on immigration. Quotas were established, which restricted most immigration from Eastern Europe. Access to Palestine as a Jewish refuge assumed greater importance.

The largest wave of Jewish immigration to Palestine occurred during the years of the Fifth Aliya. Between 1929 and 1939, 250,000 Jews arrived from Germany. With the beginning of Nazi rule in Germany in 1933, Jews experienced increasing danger to their lives, culture, and livelihoods. Many, realizing the risks they faced by remaining in Germany, began to flee.

During the years of the Great Depression, 1929 to 1941, membership in the Zionist Organization of America dropped to less than 15,000. Nonetheless, sympathy for Zionism remained high. In 1930 the British issued a White Paper (an official government position paper) halting further development of the Yishuv, the Jewish settlement in

Palestine. The White Paper sided with Arab views that increased Jewish immigration posed a danger to the Arabs living in Palestine. Reaction from Jews in the United States was swift. At a mass demonstration at New York's Madison Square Garden, 25,000 people inside the hall, and an equal number outside, heard Rabbi Wise declare, "No Jew I know has more truly the right to feel betrayed. . . ." The White Paper was never implemented, but the ability of Britain to fairly govern Palestine, put in place by the League of Nations mandate following World War I, was questioned.

Three years later Rabbi Wise organized another demonstration at Madison Square Garden. As 30,000 people milled around outside the packed hall, Jewish and non-Jewish speakers spoke against the Nazi threats to German Jews. Rabbi Wise wrote: "I cannot remember Jewry being so wrought up against anything happening to American Jews as the sudden reversion on the part of a great and cultured and liberty-loving people [the Germans] to practices which may be mildly characterized as medieval."

Alarmed at the threats to Jews around the world, American Zionism revived from its fragmented past. Organizations that had previously opposed the movement now joined with the Zionists. At their 1937 conference, Reform rabbis declared "the obligation of all Jewry to aid in [Palestine's] upbuilding as a Jewish homeland." In 1939, as Jews desperately sought refuge from Hitler's Germany, the British, bowing to Arab demands, issued another White Paper, limiting immigration of Jews to Palestine and stopping it completely in 1944. The British government, anticipating the impending war with Germany, was anxious not to offend the Arabs. An Arab uprising against the British in the Middle East could lead to closure of the Suez Canal and denial of valuable oil for the war effort. The Jewish Agency said: "It is the darkest hour of Jewish history that the British Government proposes to deprive the Jews of their last hope and to close the door to their homeland."

At a conference of American Zionists held in May 1942 at New York's Biltmore Hotel, delegates adopted the "Biltmore Program," which condemned the British White Paper as "cruel and indefensible." They also adopted a resolution calling for Palestine to be declared "a Jewish Commonwealth, integrated in the structure of the new democratic world."

In 1935, Rabbi Stephen Wise was elected leader of the Zionist Organization of America. The insecure American Jewish community did not wish to call undue attention to itself. This lack of assertiveness was called by some the "Sha! Sha! Syndrome." "Sha" is a Yiddish word meaning "keep quiet" and out of the limelight so your enemies won't have a target to attack. Wise strongly believed in the power of quiet diplomacy. He relied on his friendship with the new president of the United States, Franklin Delano Roosevelt, and State Department officials to rescue the endangered Jews of Europe. He was too optimistic.

In August 1942, Gerhardt Riegner, the Swiss representative of the World Jewish Congress, received undisputed news that the Nazis were systematically murdering the Jews of Europe. He immediately sent a telegram to Rabbi Wise through the American Embassy's diplomatic pouch, the State Department's private courier service to which President Roosevelt had given Wise access. State Department officials thought the information was unbelievable. Fearing hysterical public reaction, they withheld the telegram from Wise.

When Wise finally learned of the telegram, the State Department swore Wise to secrecy and reluctantly began an investigation to verify the information. Finally, in November, a State Department official confirmed that the mass murder of Jews was actually taking place in Europe. At a hastily called news conference, Wise released the dramatic news to reporters. The next day a short account of Wise's announcement appeared on page ten of *The New York Times*.

Several months later, at a mass rally in New York, Chaim Weizmann said, "When the historian of the future assembles the black record of our days, he will find two things unbelievable: first, the crime itself; second, the reaction of the world to that crime."

The failure of quiet diplomacy led to the rise of a new leader of American Zionists who, like Wise, was a Reform rabbi. But unlike Wise, with his belief in quiet interaction, Abba Hillel Silver called for American Jews to go public with "loud diplomacy." While Wise was willing to postpone the struggle for a Jewish state to get Jews to safety in Palestine, Silver viewed implementation of the Balfour Declaration as the major goal. In 1943, Silver and Wise were appointed cochairmen of the American Zionist Emergency Committee.

In a fiery 1943 speech, Silver told the American Jewish Committee, "We cannot truly rescue the Jews of Europe unless we have free immigration into Palestine. We cannot have free immigration into Palestine unless our political rights are recognized there. Our political rights cannot be recognized there unless our historic connection with the country is acknowledged and our rights to rebuild our national home is reaffirmed. These are inseparable links in the chain. The whole chain breaks if one of the links is missing."[8]

Silver energized the Zionist public relations campaign. Unleashing limitless press releases, mass demonstrations, letter-writing campaigns, and political activism, the Zionist cause was embraced by labor unions, state legislators, members of Congress, churches, and news organizations. Fueling support for a Jewish state were reports filtering out of Europe about the indiscriminate murder of Jews by advancing German forces.

Between 1943 and 1944, seventeen state legislatures passed resolutions supporting a Jewish homeland. Forty-one of the forty-eight state governors signed a petition to "open the doors of Palestine." The 1944 platforms of the Republican and Democratic parties called for the "opening of Palestine to . . . unrestricted immigration and land ownership. . . ."

According to the 1939 White Paper all Jewish immigration to Palestine was to end by 1944. During May 1944, hearings were held in Congress on a resolution opposing implementation of the White Paper. Nevertheless, the secretary of war called upon congressional leaders not to adopt the resolution since it would be "prejudicial to the successful prosecution of the war." Britain was, after all, America's closest ally in the fight against Germany.

President Roosevelt called Rabbis Wise and Silver to the White House and reassured them that "full justice will be done to those who seek a Jewish National Home, for which our Government and the American people have always had the deepest sympathy, and today more than ever, in view of the tragic plight of hundreds of thousands of homeless Jewish refugees."

When World War II ended, the tragedy of the Holocaust led Jews to the inescapable conclusion that it was time for a Jewish state. Abba Hillel Silver said, "If our rights are denied to us, we shall fight for them with whatever weapons are at our disposal."[9] Membership in the Zionist Organization of America rose to 500,000 by 1948, and financial contributions exceeded $200 million. Underground activities in the United States raised additional moneys for the purchase of military equipment that would be needed for the survival of a Jewish state.

At the same time, the Zionists instituted a new wave of illegal immigration to Palestine, which they called Aliya Bet. It was composed of concentration camp survivors smuggled into Palestine by ships through British naval blockades. The whole world watched the reality of a Jewish state unfolding before its eyes.

Speaking at the United Nations Peace Conference in San Francisco in May 1945, Stephen Wise spoke his mind. "The Christian world, and I include England, of course, in the Christian world, suffered six million of the people of Jesus of Nazareth to die in a most horrible manner. The Christian world owes the Jews some reparation."

1948

I never wanted him [Truman] to do anything for the oppressed Jewish people abroad if doing so would result in the slightest damage to the best interests of my country.

—Eddie Jacobson

Eddie Jacobson of Kansas City, Missouri, was the most un-likely person to deserve credit for the founding of the State of Israel in 1948. Although Jacobson was a proud and prac-ticing Jew, he did not consider himself a Zionist. He did not hold an elective position, nor was he a university professor. He was, in fact, a haberdasher—a seller of shirts, ties, and hats in his Kansas City men's furnishings store. What set Eddie Jacobson apart was his close relationship with a long-time friend with whom he had once owned another haber-dashery. The friends met early in their careers and served together in World War I: Jacobson as a sergeant and his friend as a captain. Over the years they developed the in-formal relationship of brothers. Although the friend no longer lived in Kansas City, Jacobson visited him often; no invitation was ever necessary. Eddie Jacobson's close friend was Harry S. Truman, the thirty-third president of the United States.

Following the horrors of the Holocaust, the Zionist dream of establishing an independent Jewish nation in Palestine seemed close to realization. The world, perhaps feeling some responsibility for the deaths of six million Jews by the Nazis, sympathized with the plight of desperate Jewish survivors. Hundreds of thousands of displaced persons languished in primitive camps throughout Europe. They had no homes to which they could return. Pressure mounted on Great Britain to lift the strict immigration rules it had imposed in Palestine, therefore admitting large numbers of Jews.

There was much at stake for all sides with interests in Palestine. For the Arabs, it meant sharing a single land with Jews. For Jews, it meant the fulfillment of a two-thousand-year dream of returning to their ancient homeland. World War II hastened a solution to the problem of Palestine. President Truman's personal envoy toured the displaced persons' camps in Europe and interviewed Holocaust survivors. "The civilized world," he reported to the president, "owes it [to these] survivors to provide . . . a home where they can settle down . . . to live as human beings."

On December 4, 1945, newly sworn-in president Harry Truman welcomed Chaim Weizmann to the White House. Truman was sympathetic to a solution for the desperate Jewish refugees but opposed the idea of a "Jewish" rather than a secular state. Ever an optimist, the president had hoped Arabs and Jews might join together to form a single country.

Following the meeting, Weizmann wrote a clarifying letter to reassure the president. "When we speak of a Jewish state we place no stress on the religion of the individuals who will form the majority of its inhabitants, but we have in mind a secular state based on sound democratic foundations with political machinery and institutions on the pattern of those in the United States and in Western Europe." Weizmann then directly addressed Truman's heartfelt desire to solve the refugee problem. "We believe," he wrote, "that a great deal of what is tragic in Jewish history is the result of that hopelessness." President Truman responded by issuing a futile appeal to Great Britain to allow 100,000 Jewish refugees to enter Palestine.

While the diplomatic efforts continued, a highly organized large-scale movement began of illegal immigrants from Europe's displaced persons' camps to Palestine. Jewish defense groups such as the Irgun and the Stern Gang escalated violence against the British, while Arab attacks on Jews grew in intensity. The British, unable to control the situation, announced plans to withdraw from Palestine in May 1948 and end their thirty-year administration.

Attention turned to the United Nations, where debate was ongoing on plans to partition Palestine between Jews and Arabs. As the world's major post-World War II power, the United States' support of partition was important. Zionists feared that pro-Arab feelings in the State Department would tilt American policy against a Jewish state. American Jews and Zionist leaders mobilized a public relations campaign to influence the opinions of governmental leaders. Mass demonstrations in favor of a Jewish state were held throughout the country. Support came from Christians and Jews and resulted in thousands of letters and telegrams to members of Congress and the president. Governors of 37 states, 33 state legislatures, 54 U.S. senators, and 250 congressmen all notified the president of their support for a Jewish homeland.

As political and diplomatic efforts intensified, attention turned to President Truman. On his shoulders alone rested the possibility of a Jewish homeland. But Harry Truman was a stubborn man; he did not like to be pushed, and American Jews were relentless in their ongoing campaign for his support. A United Nations committee voted to sup-

Eddie Jacobson, a men's clothing salesman from Kansas City, Missouri, was living proof that it helps to have friends in high places. Jacobson was enlisted by supporters of Zionism to use his influence with his friend, President Harry Truman, in the quest for a Jewish homeland. Jacobson (left) and Truman are shown in Jacobson's store.

port partition of Palestine into Jewish and Arab lands. Its reasoning was clear: "There are now in Palestine some 650,000 Jews and some 1,200,000 Arabs who are dissimilar in their ways of living and, for the time being, separated by political interests which render difficult full and effective political cooperation among them." The holy cities of Jerusalem and Bethlehem were to be administered by the United Nations.

The partition plan then went to the General Assembly for a final and decisive vote. For most of November 1947 the members of the United Nations debated the issue. Maps of Palestine were drawn and redrawn. One of the areas of debate was the Negev Desert, a seemingly useless, barren area, which the world powers were initially inclined to give to the Jews. Arab leaders objected and UN members began to rethink that idea. As Thanksgiving approached, the United States had to take a public stand on the specifics of a partition plan.

Harry Truman was growing testy on the explosive subject of Palestine. Chaim Weizmann was in New York to be on hand for the United Nations vote. On November 18 he took the train to Washington for a secret meeting with President Truman. Weizmann was met at the station by Supreme Court Justice Felix Frankfurter, who escorted him to his hotel. Later that day, after being led into the White House through a private entrance, away from the view of reporters, Weizmann met briefly with the president. The elder Jewish statesman refrained from repeating the often heard political arguments. Instead, he dramatically spread a map on a table and told the president about the great potential of the barren Negev Desert in the south of Palestine to bloom under Jewish care. Weizmann had heard about the rumblings on the diplomatic scene that the Negev might be ceded to the Arabs. Truman was so impressed with Weizmann's argument that he made a commitment to support the Negev as a Jewish area.

Eddie Jacobson had also been visiting the president. Months earlier, learning about the haberdasher's relationship with the president, an official of B'nai Brith, the Jewish fraternal society, called fellow member Jacobson. Could Eddie speak with his friend about seeking admission to Palestine of 100,000 desperate displaced Jews still languishing in Europe? "Harry Truman will do what's right if he knows the facts," Jacobson told his caller. "If I can help supply them, I will. But I am no Zionist, so first I need the facts from you."[1]

Jacobson contacted his friend. In a letter to the president, Jacobson appealed "in behalf of my People:"

> The future of one and one-half million Jews in Europe depends on what happens at the present meeting of the United Nations. . . . I think I am one of few who actually knows and realizes what terrible heavy burdens you are carrying on your shoulders during these hectic days. I should, therefore, be the last man to add to them: but I feel you will forgive me for doing so, because tens of thousands of lives depend on words from your mouth and heart. Harry, my people need help and I am appealing to you to help them.[2]

As the United Nation's vote on partition approached, Jacobson made several private visits to the White House.

On November 29, 1947, the General Assembly of the United Nations voted thirty-three for, thirteen against, and ten abstaining for the partition of Palestine into two states, one Jewish and one Arab. "It was because the White House was for it that it went through," one insider said. Eddie Jacobson later recounted that Truman said "he [Truman] and he alone was responsible for swinging the votes of several delegations." In his diary Jacobson wrote two words for November 29—"Mission accomplished."

"The vote in the United Nations is only the beginning," Truman wrote. He understood that the new Jewish nation faced great dangers from Arab retaliation in the days ahead. After joyous celebrations in the streets of Tel Aviv, Jews prepared for an intensified wave of Arab-generated violence in Palestine. The British were prepared to do as little as possible to keep the peace in Palestine so as not to endanger the lives of their soldiers. They still planned to withdraw from Palestine six months later, on May 15, 1948. With time of the essence, and violence escalating, Zionists in the United States intensified the political pressure. The first battle for recognition had been won; the next could result in the first Jewish independent state after nearly two thousand years.

Anti-Zionist feelings in the United States government endangered the future of the partition plan. State Department officials strongly favored a United Nations trusteeship of Palestine. They feared that U.S. support of partition would anger Arab countries who might cut off supplies of oil. In February 1948 the U.S. ambassador to the United Nations announced that the partition plan was unenforceable. He declared that once the British left, the combined armies of five Arab countries would sweep into Palestine and "drive the Jews into the sea."

While the president fought with his own diplomats, Jewish leaders heightened the tension by announcing their intention to declare an independent Jewish state the moment the British mandate ended. The new country would not have a chance of survival without international recognition, particularly from the United States.

In 1947, 1948, and 1949, the White House received 86,500 letters, 841,903 postcards, and 51,400 telegrams on the Palestine issue. Truman's stubbornness worsened as the pressure on him increased. He refused to listen to anyone about the Palestine issue. "I do not think that I ever had so much pressure and propaganda at the White House as I had in this instance," Truman later noted. He turned down all requests for appointments dealing with Palestine. The exasperated president wrote: "What I am trying to do is make the whole world safe for the Jews. Therefore I don't feel like going to war in Palestine."

The supporters of a Jewish state felt that all might be lost unless Chaim Weizmann could meet with and influence the president once again. But no one could convince the president to see the aging Jewish leader. Eddie Jacobson received yet another telephone call from Frank Goldman, the national president of B'nai Brith, and Jacobson wrote another letter to his friend in the White House. Jacobson urged Truman to see Weizmann. Truman refused, saying the entire Palestine problem was "not solvable as presently set up." Jacobson packed a suitcase and headed for Washington.

On arriving at the White House on Saturday, March 12, 1948, Jacobson entered the president's office, as he often did, without an appointment. After some casual and friendly banter, the haberdasher brought up the subject of Palestine. Truman's demeanor suddenly changed. His words were few, his manner angry. "He never talked to me in this manner or in any way even approaching it," Jacobson later recounted. Jacobson reminded Truman "of his [Truman's] feelings for Dr. Weizmann." Jacobson raised one argument after another. The president, however, was not moved. He could only speak of the "disrespectful and mean" way certain Jews in the United States had treated him in their zeal for a Jewish state. Jacobson sadly thought that "my dear friend, the President of the United States, was at that moment as close to being an anti-Semite as a man could possibly be."[3]

With nothing more to add, Jacobson caught a glimpse of a bronze statue of Andrew Jackson against the wall. "Harry," Jacobson said, "all your life you had a hero. You are probably the best read man in America on the life of

Andrew Jackson. . . .Well, Harry, I too have a hero, a man I never met, but who is, I think, the greatest Jew who ever lived . . . he is a sick man, almost broken in health, but he traveled thousands and thousands of miles just to see you and plead the cause of my people. Now you refuse to see him because you were insulted by some of our American Jewish leaders. . . . It doesn't sound like you, Harry. . . . I wouldn't be here if I didn't know that, if you will see him, you will be properly and accurately informed on the situation as it exists in Palestine, and yet you refuse to see him."

The room was silent. Slowly, through tear-filled eyes, Jacobson noticed that the president was drumming on his desk with his fingers. Truman then turned his swivel chair toward the window and stared out into the rose garden for what seemed to Jacobson like an eternity. Suddenly, the president turned around, looked directly at his old friend and blurted, "You win, you baldheaded [expletive]. I will see him. . . ."

Jacobson was emotionally drained. On his way back to the hotel where Frank Goldman anxiously awaited word of the meeting, Jacobson stopped at the hotel bar. For the first time in his life he ordered and quickly downed two double bourbons. When he finally entered the room and relayed the good news to Goldman, the B'nai Brith president embraced and kissed him!

Five days later, out of sight of reporters, Chaim Weizmann was again secretly escorted into the White House. Truman did not even notify the State Department. For three quarters of an hour, President Truman and Dr. Weizmann met privately. Truman assured the Zionist leader of his support of the partition plan and the inclusion of the Negev in the Jewish state. "And when he left my office," Truman later wrote, "I felt that he had received a full understanding of my policy and that I knew what it was he wanted."

The very next morning, without any warning to Truman, Ambassador Warren Austin told the United Nations that the United States recommended abandoning the partition plan and called for a temporary UN "trusteeship" over Palestine. Just a day earlier Truman had personally assured Chaim Weizmann of continued United States support for partition. Eddie Jacobson felt betrayed. Jewish leaders were furious. The president was angrier than them all. His support of partition had been publicly refuted by his own ambassador. He felt humiliated and dishonored. "The State Department pulled the rug from under me today," Truman raged in his diary. "This morning I find that the State Department has reversed my Palestine policy. I am now in the position of a liar and double-crosser. I've never felt so in my life. There are people on the third and fourth levels of the State Dept. who have always wanted to cut my throat."[4]

Chaim Weizmann called Eddie Jacobson and told him not to "be disappointed and do not feel badly." Weizmann said he did not believe that President Truman realized what his UN ambassador would say. He also urged Jacobson not to "forget for a single moment that Harry S. Truman is the most powerful single man in the world. You have a job to do; so keep the White House doors open."[5] Weizmann wrote a heartfelt letter to Truman. "The choice for our people, Mr. President, is between statehood and extermination. History and providence have placed this issue in your hands and I am confident that you will decide it in the spirit of the moral law."

Debate continued at the highest levels of government in Washington. The president listened to representatives of the State Department argue against recognition of the impending state. Even his closest advisers did not know what Truman's ultimate decision might be. At a news conference a reporter asked the president what he would do.

The first president of Israel, Chaim Weizmann,
presents President Truman with a Torah on
May 25, 1948, shortly after the recognition of the
newly established Jewish state by the United States.

Truman bluntly answered, "I will cross that bridge when I get to it."

As the day approached for the British withdrawal, violence escalated in Palestine. Fund-raising for Israel picked up in the United States as representatives of the soon-to-be Jewish nation scrounged for airplanes, tanks, and guns to defend themselves once independence was declared. An arms embargo prevented arms shipments from the United States to any Middle Eastern nation.

On May 14, 1948, as the combined armies of five Arab nations encircled it, the Jews of Palestine formally accepted the United Nations partition plan and declared the establishment of the State of Israel to become effective at midnight. Eleven minutes after the new country's independence began, the United States issued a statement announcing official recognition of Israel.

> This government has been informed that a Jewish state has been proclaimed in Palestine, and recognition has been requested by the provisional government thereof. The United States recognizes the provisional government as the de facto authority of the new State of Israel.

Later that evening, President Truman received a telegram from his friend Eddie Jacobson. "Thanks," the message read, "and God bless you."

Chaim Weizmann returned to the White House on May 25, 1948, as president of the world's youngest nation. This time he did not have to be secretly escorted into the building. A motorcade carried him proudly down Pennsylvania Avenue as newly prepared flags of the Jewish state fluttered from the lampposts. In a public ceremony on the White House portico, Weizmann presented President Truman with a most meaningful gift—a scroll of the Torah, the Five Books of Moses.

1956

To stand before the United Nations and say we will withdraw—that was not my finest hour.

—Golda Meir

Israel's chances for survival were less than promising. As British troops withdrew from Palestine on May 14, 1948, the armies of Egypt, Jordan, Syria, Lebanon, and Iraq invaded the newly declared Jewish state. Woefully equipped, the army of Israel succeeded in holding back the well-equipped and trained Arab forces. The American arms embargo had hindered efforts to equip Israel's armed forces. The Israelis had less than a dozen small planes from which homemade bombs could only be dropped by hand. The fight for survival was fierce and determined. The Israelis had no alternative; they had no other place to go.

In the United States, Israeli operatives used innovative, if illegal, methods to obtain American arms to save Israel from a premature death. Working with sympathetic leaders of organized crime and labor unions, they were able to ship desperately needed ammunition, parts, and equipment from major ports on the East Coast.

Help came from some unlikely sources. Frank Sinatra was one of America's favorite singers. He was also committed to the survival of Israel. The story is told that once, while performing at the legendary Copacabana Club in New York City, Sinatra came to the aid of Israel in an imaginative way: The headquarters of the Israeli agents, in the same building as the club, were under constant surveillance by the Federal Bureau of Investigation (FBI). A ship filled with illegal arms bound for Israel was stalled at the dock—the captain refused to set sail until he was paid. Unable to leave the building undetected, the Israelis turned to Sinatra. When an Israeli walked out the front door as a decoy, the FBI agents followed. Meanwhile, Sinatra, carrying a suitcase filled with thousands of dollars in cash, went out the back door unnoticed and headed for the docks. The captain was paid and the ship sailed that night with guns and ammunition for the beleaguered Israeli fighters.

Hundreds of thousands of Arab residents of Palestine fled the fighting by crossing into neighboring Arab lands. They hoped for a quick return once the Israelis had been defeated. Instead, they were to languish permanently in hastily constructed refugee camps under the supervision of the United Nations as displaced persons unable to return to their former homes. While Jewish refugees who were expelled from Arab lands were welcomed and absorbed in Israel, Palestinian refugees were unassimilated by neighboring Arab nations. The seemingly unsolvable issue of Palestinian refugees would concern every American president from then on.

For Israeli Prime Minister Ben-Gurion, the absorption of Jewish immigrants was a prime concern. He had arrived in Palestine from Russia in 1906 as part of the Second Aliya and quickly became a leader of the Jewish settlement. In April 1948, as head of the People's Council, he proclaimed to the world the establishment of the State of Israel and became the country's first prime minister. Ben-Gurion was sympathetically described in one American news magazine as "an Old Testament patriarch." A newspaper, referring to Ben-Gurion's humble beginnings, declared that "the strengthened hands of a laborer will hold the reins of government."[1]

In a draft of a top-secret telegram to Ben-Gurion, Harry Truman warned, "The U.S. is seriously disturbed by the attitude of Israel with respect to a territorial settlement in Palestine and to the question of Palestinian refugees. . . . The U.S. government and people have given generous support to the creation of Israel because they have been convinced of the justice of this aspiration." In the telegram, the president stated his concern that Israel's attitude endangered relations between Israel and its neighbors and could lead to a "revision of [United States] attitude toward Israel."[2] Meanwhile, Egypt and Jordan took advantage of the fighting and diplomatic debates to occupy territory originally earmarked by the United Nations for an Arab Palestinian state: Jordan ruled over the West Bank including the Old City of Jerusalem, while Egypt controlled the Gaza Strip.

On May 11, 1949, the UN General Assembly approved Israel's membership as the fifty-ninth member of the United Nations. After a series of broken truces, Israel signed armistice agreements in 1949 that put an end to the fighting. The Jewish state found itself in possession of nearly 25 percent more territory than had originally been allocated to it by the United Nations. But armistice only meant a cease-fire, not a permanent peace. The Arab nations refused to acknowledge the existence of Israel. They imposed economic boycotts and barred Israeli shipping from international waterways under their control, including the Suez Canal.

As Arab nations spoke about their eventual "liberation of Palestine," the United States, France, and Great Britain issued a joint Tripartite Declaration, which pledged action by the three powers, "if necessary, to prevent any violation of frontiers or armistice lines." But the lofty words could not prevent Egypt from denying passage to Israeli shipping through the Suez Canal or blocking use of the Straits of Tiran to ships headed for Israel's southern port of Eilat.

The first task of the new nation was the biblical fulfillment of the ingathering of Jewish exiles. From displaced persons' camps in Europe came more than 100,000 survivors of the Nazi Holocaust. From Arab lands such as Yemen and Iraq came other Jews expelled from the only homes they had known for centuries. Between 1949 and 1951 more than 600,000 Jewish immigrants arrived in Israel. Among them were fewer than 2,000 American Jews.

The vast majority of Jews in the United States were committed to the survival of the new Jewish state. They drew the line, however, at "making Aliya," or returning to their ancient homeland. They may not have emigrated, but in economic and political ways, their support was invaluable. Within a decade of Israel's founding, there were no less than eighteen major American Jewish organizations dedicated to Israel's support.

To coordinate activities and avoid duplication of efforts, three "umbrella" organizations were created: the American Zionist Council, the National Community Relations Advisory Council, and the Conference of Presidents of Major Jewish Organizations. In effect, they created a politically powerful network to advocate for Israel in Washington. The fact that American Jews were concentrated in major population areas such as New York, Baltimore, Boston, and Philadelphia, and that they tended to vote in greater proportion than most other citizens, contributed to the myth of the all-powerful "Jewish vote." In actuality, Jews comprised less than 3 percent of the American population, but politicians decided they could not ignore Jewish concern for Israel.

The pro-Israel attitude in the United States extended beyond the Jewish community. In a 1952 address to members of a Boston synagogue, Congressman John F. Kennedy spoke of the contrasts he felt during two trips he had taken to Israel. After his first visit in 1939 he "came away with a feeling of hopelessness for the future." During a 1951 visit he met with Prime Minister David Ben-Gurion. "While private philanthropy and private investment can help make Israel economically self-sufficient," Kennedy told the pro-Israel audience, "the United Nations and our own country also have a role to play. I was glad to see the American Congress recognize last summer that this Israeli policy deserved American support and I was happy to support the appropriation of fifty million dollars for this purpose. For the peace of the world it is important that the Arab States recognize the reality of the existence of Israel. Israel is here to stay."[3]

Speaking in 1958, former President Harry Truman said, "The State of Israel was set up as a homeland and place of refuge for one of the most cruelly treated minorities in world history . . . we believed in the justice of Israel's cause when the State of Israel was created. That cause is no less just today."[4]

In the 1950s, Americans were humming the Israeli song "Tzena, Tzena," which was heard over radio stations across America. The book *Exodus* by Leon Uris sold more than four million copies after its 1958 publication. Its dramatic and sympathetic portrayal of Israel's founding colored Americans' views of the Jewish state and its people, especially after it was turned into a popular feature film in 1960.

Fund-raising for Israel became a primary concern of the American Jewish community. Between 1946 and 1962 more than $1 billion was raised through the United Jewish Appeal (UJA), the central fund-raising agency for Israel. Israel Bonds were established in 1951. Since then, more than $10 billion worth of bonds have been sold.

*The 1951 visit to Israel of John F. Kennedy (right) was
the beginning of a meaningful relationship between the
young Massachusetts congressman, later president of
the United States, and the young country. Here, Kennedy
meets with Prime Minister David Ben-Gurion (left) and
fellow congressman Franklin Roosevelt, Jr. (center).*

Funds raised through the sale of bonds are used to build
Israel's highways, power plants, seaports, and pipelines and
to support high-technology research.

From the beginning, U.S. economic aid was vital to Israel. In January 1949 the United States extended a $100-
million export-import bank loan to the emerging country
for the purchase of needed agricultural material. Additional
funds followed on a yearly basis until the mid-1950s.

While the economy of the new country was of concern,
greater interest focused on military threats to its existence.
Even after armistice agreements were signed in 1949, attacks

by fedayeen, or armed guerrillas, across the newly established borders continued to take Jewish lives. These commando groups, trained and financed by Egypt, Jordan, and Syria, hoped to weaken Israel's resolve. The goal of the fedayeen raids was to wear down the morale of Israelis. They hoped Israel would become so fearful that it would ultimately accept the 1947 borders originally proposed by the United Nations but spurned at that time by the Arabs. When asked whether or not Arab states might not fear aggression by Israel, Prime Minister David Ben-Gurion told Congressman John F. Kennedy, "How could a country like Egypt, with a population of twenty million, fear invasion by a small nation of less than two million?"

The United Nations was unable and the Arab countries unwilling to halt the growing number of thefts, sabotage, and armed clashes. Between 1949 and 1953 more than 175 Jews, mainly civilians, were killed in such attacks. Many more were wounded, and damage to agricultural and construction equipment mounted.

In response to terrorist raids, Israel's army retaliated against targets in Jordan and Egypt. Between January and September 1953, the United Nations recorded more than one thousand border raids from Jordan. The world remained silent. At the United Nations, Israel's complaints about attacks on its citizens were largely ignored. On the evening of October 12, 1953, Arab infiltrators crossed the Jordanian border and entered the Israeli settlement of Moshav Yahud. A hand grenade thrown into a house caused the deaths of two small children and their mother. Two nights later Israel retaliated. A unit of the Israeli army crossed into Jordan and entered the village of Qibya, where they believed guerrilla activity was centered. There, the troops destroyed forty houses and killed fifty civilians. The world was indignant.

The United States immediately denounced the attack. At the United Nations, Israel was roundly condemned and officially reprimanded by the Security Council. A censure resolution called on Israel "to take effective measures to prevent all such action in the future." At the same time, the United Nations simply "requested" Jordan to "prevent all such actions in the future" that could lead to Israeli response. The one-sided condemnation of Israel became a way of life at the United Nations as the Security Council "consistently refused to differentiate" between Arab attacks and Israel's responses.

Abba Eban, Israel's ambassador to the United States, defended Israel's situation. "The whole of Israel is a frontier," he said. "The Arab governments refuse to live in peace with Israel; and they also refuse to let Israel live in peace." Eban explained that Jordan and Egypt encouraged guerrilla attacks from their territories "to undermine Israel's morale, paralyze its economy, and inflict as many casualties as possible."[5] His words fell on deaf ears. With the 9–0 passage of the censure motion against Israel, Eban complained that "no censure whatever—strong, moderate or mild—was seen fit to be applied by the Security Council to the Arab murder of hundreds of Israelis before the deplorable action at Qibya."[6] Although censure motions had no practical impact on Israel, they embarrassed and isolated Israel within the world community.

The guerrilla attacks did not stop. On March 17, 1954, fedayeen from across the Jordanian border attacked a civilian bus in the Negev, killing eleven passengers. A few days earlier, in the North, Syrian gunners had fired on Israeli fishing boats on the Sea of Galilee.

Relations with the United States were at a low ebb. The Qibya incident resulted in a temporary suspension by the United States of $26 million in economic aid to Israel. To compound the situation, Israel formally moved its Foreign Ministry from Tel Aviv to its declared capital of Jerusalem. Most countries, including the United States, considered the move a contravention of the 1947 UN partition resolution,

*Israel's early years were marked by violence at the hands of
its bitter enemies and neighbors in the Middle East.
Meetings such as this one between Israeli Prime Minister
Ben-Gurion (center), Ambassador Abba Eban (right),
and President Truman were instrumental in maintaining
relations between Israel and the United States, thereby
helping to ensure Israel's survival.*

which set Jerusalem apart as an international city. Israel, however, considered Jerusalem its capital and shifted its governmental operations there.

When in 1955, Israel embarked on a massive hydro-electric power project involving the construction of a canal to divert water from the Jordan River, Arab countries protested. The United Nations intervened to stop the work. The United States response was again to withhold economic aid to Israel. Israel felt that the United States was applying a double standard to Israel by not considering the reasons for Israel's actions. Relations between Israel and the United States had taken a turn for the worse with the election of President Dwight David Eisenhower in 1952. Although support of Israel continued initially, John Foster Dulles, Eisenhower's secretary of state, formulated a policy of "friendly impartiality" toward the Middle East. Dulles feared the spread of Soviet influence around the world and wanted to prevent the Arab nations from tilting toward communism.

Beginning in 1954, there was a dramatic increase in the number of guerrilla attacks on Israel from bases in Egypt and the Egyptian-controlled Gaza Strip. Early in 1955, Israel responded by attacking an Egyptian military camp in Gaza. Again, the United Nations quickly censured Israel but failed to recognize the guerrilla actions by Arabs that had forced Israel's response. "There comes a time," wrote an American Jewish Committee correspondent in Israel, "when drastic action is needed to deal with an intolerable situation." The United States firmly declared its opposition to "any policy of reprisal or retaliation." In March 1955, Israel was unanimously censured by the Security Council, which declared Israel's actions "indefensible from any standpoint." U.S. Ambassador Henry Cabot Lodge, Jr., said, "Whatever the provocation might have been in this case, there was no justification for the Israeli military action at Gaza."

"To my regret," David Ben-Gurion later wrote, "for some time the United Nations authorities had shown an inclination to transform the Armistice Agreement into a one-sided obligation on our part toward the United Nations, absolving the other signatories."[7]

Most American Jews were frustrated with the seeming lack of American government understanding of Israel's problems. The Eisenhower administration did not initially grasp the deep feelings held by most American Jews for Israel. The president and his advisers had close ties with the American Council for Judaism, an organization opposed to Zionism, which represented a tiny fraction of American Jews. American supporters of Israel turned to other political arenas for support.

In January 1954 the America-Israel Society was formed to "foster good will and promote cultural relations between the United States and Israel." Among the influential founders of the Society were the governors of Massachusetts, New Jersey, and Michigan; Supreme Court Justice Felix Frankfurter; Mrs. Eleanor Roosevelt; senators and members of Congress; and leaders of industry, education, and the arts. Eventually, the Eisenhower administration realized that the American Council for Judaism was not representative of American Jews.

When Israel submitted a request to the U.S. government for additional arms, the president said the request would be "considered sympathetically." It soon became clear that the supply of arms from the United States clearly tilted toward the Arab countries. When the U.S. government proposed in 1954 to supply arms to Iraq and Saudi Arabia, Israeli Ambassador Abba Eban objected that both Arab countries had not even concluded a formal armistice and continued to publicly declare their intentions to destroy Israel. "It would be a most inopportune moment," Eban stated, ". . . to strengthen the military equipment of any member of the Arab League."[8] But the United States was more concerned about its balance of power in the Middle East with the Soviet Union. The fight against communism and America's increased dependence on oil from that region tilted American foreign policy toward the Arabs. American Jewish organizations, among others, protested to Washington. In Israel many felt that the United States had abandoned all but a pretense of neutrality.[9]

In April and May 1954, Henry A. Byroade, assistant secretary of state, delivered major speeches in which he called upon Israel to "come truly to look upon yourselves as a Middle Eastern State . . . rather than as the headquarters . . . of a worldwide grouping of peoples of a particular faith who must have special rights and obligations within the State of Israel." In effect, he urged Israel to repudiate its existence as a Jewish state and its fundamental Law of Return, which assures Jews who desire to settle in Israel the right to do so. Byroade's words, together with the ongoing Arab economic and diplomatic boycotts of Israel, and escalating guerrilla war, brought Israel to the end of its patience. Ben-Gurion told the Knesset, Israel's parliament, on November 2, 1955, "If our rights are violated by acts of violence on land or at sea, we shall preserve freedom of action to defend our rights in the most effective manner possible."[10]

In 1952 a group of disgruntled army officers had overthrown King Farouk of Egypt. After an internal power struggle, Colonel Gamal Abdel Nasser, an Egyptian nationalist, emerged as president. His goal was to unite the Arab world into an unaligned political force on the world scene. He began by demonstrating his independence from the United States. In 1955 the United States created the Baghdad Pact, an anti-Communist defense treaty linking Iraq, Turkey, Pakistan, Iran, and Britain. Nasser, angry at what he viewed as outside encroachment on the Arab world, worked to overthrow the Western-backed governments of Iraq and Jordan.

His anti-Western actions did not prevent him from turning to the West for economic and military aid, however. The United States agreed to Nasser's 1955 request for military equipment but insisted on cash payment. Egypt did not have the cash and turned to the Soviet Union instead. In return for Egyptian cotton, the Soviets provided Nasser with five times more military gear than he would have received from the United States.[11] The arms agreement was just what the Soviets had long wanted: a presence in the Middle East.

Nasser also adopted a hard-line attitude toward Israel, resulting in increased fedayeen attacks and strident propaganda. "The day of Israel's destruction approaches," one Radio Cairo broadcast blared. "There shall be no peace on the borders, for we demand vengeance and vengeance means death to Israel."[12] Similar threats came from Jordan. "The time has come," a Jordanian military leader said, "when the Arabs will be able to choose the time for an offensive to liquidate Israel."[13] Israel felt even more isolated.

With tensions high, President Eisenhower advised Israel to soften its attitude toward its neighbors. Eisenhower denied Israel's request for additional arms because "it would only speed a Middle East arms race."[14] In a letter to Prime Minister Ben-Gurion, the president implored Israel to make territorial concessions to Jordan and Egypt. Secretary of State Dulles suggested that Israel give up the Negev. "I sincerely hope," Eisenhower continued, "you will abstain from any retaliatory acts which may result in very dangerous consequences."[15] An angry Ben-Gurion responded publicly in a speech marking Israel's Independence Day. "The conscience of the Great Powers failed," he thundered, "when Hitler sent six million Jews of Europe to the Slaughter. Will that conscience fail again?"[16] Israel was disappointed that it could no longer trust America to stand up and fight for Western interests. Instead, Israel turned to other sources, including Britain, France, and Canada, for arms with which to defend itself.

Colonel Gamal Abdel Nasser was a foe of Israel's from the time he assumed power of Egypt in 1952. He also resented the encroachment on the Arab world by the United States when in 1955 it created the Baghdad Pact, a treaty drawn up to prevent the spread of communism in the Middle East.

In the attempt to maintain a neutral stance in the Middle East, the United States concentrated on implied Soviet threats to the region and ignored Israel's real concerns with ongoing attacks from its neighbors. Speaking at a 1955 Washington conference of governmental and Jewish leaders, John D. Jernegan, the deputy assistant secretary of state for the Near East, presented a naive view of Israel's situation. "I should like to say," Jernegan said, "that in my opinion Israel as a nation is not in danger . . . she is not directly in the path of possible Soviet aggression. . . . What is more important, I do not see evidence of any intent on the part of her neighbors to attack Israel." Although a Soviet attack on Israel was unlikely, the Soviet Union adopted a harsh anti-Israel policy. Soviet Prime Minister Nikita Khrushchev said, "From the beginning Israel has adopted a hostile and threatening attitude toward its neighbors. The imperialists [the United States and Western European countries] stand behind Israel and try to use her as a tool against the Arabs for their own ends." Khrushchev's words did not comfort Israel and encouraged Nasser.

During the first few months of 1956, the border situation in the south of Israel deteriorated. At the end of March, Nasser massed troops in the Sinai and by early April had begun preparations for an actual attack. He escalated the tension by increasing fedayeen attacks on Israeli civilian buses, homes, and pipelines. Each succeeding Egyptian attack resulted in Israeli retaliation.

The world remained indifferent to Israel's problems. Egypt closed the Gulf of Aqaba to Israeli shipping. Jordan denied Jews of all countries access to Jewish holy places in East Jerusalem and the West Bank. When Israel retaliated against a particularly bloody fedayeen attack from Jordan, Britain actually threatened to intervene militarily on Jordan's side.

Meanwhile, relations between Egypt and the United States worsened. The building of the Aswan High Dam was to be more than a marvel of modern engineering. When completed, it would be a source of economic growth and prestige for Egypt, a country regularly plagued by floods and poverty. Originally funded by the United States and Britain, Nasser's arms deal with the Soviet Union resulted in the withdrawal of that funding. In direct retaliation, Nasser seized and nationalized the Suez Canal in July 1956 and several months later closed it to all Israeli shipping. The Canal had been built as an international waterway and was owned by the French and British, who reacted angrily. President Eisenhower urged Britain and France not to intervene militarily. "The United States," Eisenhower said, "is committed to a peaceful solution." Secretary of State Dulles added that the United States would not "try to shoot its way through the Canal."[17]

But Britain and France could not ignore this challenge. They secretly planned with Israel to seize the Canal from Egypt and destabilize the Nasser regime. War rumors abounded as fedayeen attacks on Israel from Egypt and Jordan escalated and Soviet military equipment poured into Egypt. "Israelis do not want war," an observer wrote. "They want to develop their country undisturbed and in peace. But they cannot sit by and watch their enemies swear that they will destroy them, while they get the arms to do it."[18]

On October 27, Israel began mobilizing its troops. United States intelligence reports indicated Jordan as the likely target of an attack. "Make it very clear to the Israelis," Eisenhower told Dulles, "that they must stop these attacks against the borders of Jordan." David Ben-Gurion responded firmly to President Eisenhower saying that if Israel did not "take all possible measures to thwart the declared aim of the Arab rulers to destroy Israel, it would not be fulfilling its elementary responsibilities." Two days later Israel surprised the United States by invading Egyptian-held Sinai and Gaza. In one hundred hours, Israel totally defeated the Egyptian army in Sinai and reached the banks of the Suez Canal. To complete the mission, Israel seized and occupied the islands from which Egypt had closed shipping through the Gulf of Aqaba to the Israeli port of Eilat.

Then, in accordance with the prearranged plan with Israel, Britain and France issued an ultimatum for Egypt and Israel to withdraw from the Suez Canal area and allow Britain and France to occupy it. Israel, of course, agreed at once; Egypt refused. On November 5, British and French forces landed in Port Said, at the entrance of the Canal, as Egypt sank ships to block the Suez Canal to all traffic. President Eisenhower was not just surprised at the invasion—he was furious. He had not expected America's closest allies, Britain and France, to ignore his wishes.

The president was particularly angry with Israel and issued a tough warning. He threatened to suspend not only government economic aid to Israel but also to restrict all private funds raised through the sale of Israel Bonds and contributions to the United Jewish Appeal. Israel, shocked by the president's threats, had other reasons to worry. It also feared direct military intervention on Egypt's behalf by sympathetic nations including the Soviet Union, India, and some African states.

At the United Nations, U.S. Ambassador Henry Cabot Lodge, Jr., expressed his "shock" at the invasion and called for the Security Council to order a cease-fire. Britain and France exercised their veto rights and the motion failed. The Soviet Union flexed its military muscle in support of Nasser, even threatening nuclear war. Escalation into a larger war loomed as the world looked on nervously. Eisenhower insisted on strong support for treaty commitments. Ambassador Lodge introduced a resolution in the General Assembly ordering an immediate cease-fire and the withdrawal of British, French, and Israeli armed forces.

In a speech to the General Assembly broadcast throughout the United States, Israeli Ambassador Abba Eban forcefully defended his country's actions. "Egypt has practiced belligerency against Israel by land. Egypt has practiced belligerency against Israel by sea." Then, referring to cross-border shelling of Israeli farmland and the denial of shipping access to Israel's port of Eilat, Eban continued, "Every citizen of Israel is entitled to till every inch of Israel's soil and to navigate every yard of Israel's waters. . . ." His words were in vain. With the General Assembly immune from Security Council member veto, the resolution passed and the invasion was stopped. Withdrawal, however, was another matter.

President Eisenhower spoke over television to the American people. He declared that the United States wanted an even-handed relationship with Arabs and Israelis and declared U.S. support for the United Nations and the rule of law. Britain and France agreed to withdraw, subject to the arrival of a United Nations Emergency Force (UNEF) to guarantee the right of free passage through the Canal. By December 22, 1956, British and French troops were gone. Israel had agreed to withdraw from captured territory except the Gaza Strip and Sharm al-Sheikh, at the tip of the Sinai, from which Egypt had previously blocked Israeli shipping. Israel would not leave until additional UN forces were stationed there.

With Israel still reluctant to withdraw, President Eisenhower spoke forcefully of his continued support of the strict rule of international law and all United Nations resolutions. He continued to exert diplomatic pressure on Israel. A disregard of the UN would "almost certainly lead to further UN action which will seriously damage relations between Israel and UN members, including the United States," he warned Ben-Gurion. When Secretary Dulles announced that the United States was seriously considering the imposition of economic sanctions on Israel through the United Nations, Israel's supporters in the United States responded with rallies and telegrams to Congress. The American Jewish community was united as never before in an all-out push on Israel's behalf. At first, American public opinion supported Eisenhower's tough stance with Israel. "Israel was no longer viewed as fighting for survival but perceived as using force for the sake of territorial aggrandizement."[19] Ben-Gurion responded forcefully to Eisenhower's demands. "Israel, though small," he said, "is entitled to security, freedom and equal rights in the family of nations. Like any other independent nation . . . our people are determined to defend their independence."[20] Within a few days American sympathy shifted, as did the attitude toward Israel in Congress and the press.

When asked how the United States could so forcefully lean on Israel while ignoring the Soviet Union's continual flouting of international law, President Eisenhower responded, "There can be no equating of a nation like Israel with that of the Soviet Union. The peoples of Israel, like those of the United States, are imbued with a religious faith and a sense of moral values." Lyndon Johnson, then the Senate majority leader, called upon the president to provide security guarantees to Israel, the small country surrounded by the more powerful Arab nations. "The United Nations," Johnson wrote, "could not apply one rule for the strong and another for the weak."

On February 11 the United States formally issued a commitment to Israel that United Nations peacekeeping forces would be stationed at Sharm al-Sheikh to secure the rights of Israeli shipping through the Gulf of Aqaba and halt fedayeen attacks from the Gaza Strip. "The United States believes," the formal guarantee stated, "that the Gulf of Aqaba constitutes international waters and that no nation has the right to forcibly prevent free and innocent passage in the Gulf and through the Straits giving access thereto." Ben-Gurion told Eisenhower that Israel would reluctantly withdraw only because the United States had assured Israel "it would have no cause to regret" leaving the occupied territory.

Golda Meir, Israel's foreign minister, addressed the United Nations General Assembly. "The Government of Israel is now in a position to announce its plans for full and prompt withdrawal from the Sharm al-Sheikh area and the Gaza Strip." Israel would withdraw, she stated, "on condition that UNEF are placed in Gaza and withdraws from Sharm al-Sheikh in the confidence that there will be continued freedom of navigation for international and Israeli shipping in the Gulf and the Straits of Tiran." The crisis was over, at least temporarily. Nonetheless, Israel's security concerns continued.

Congress approved the Eisenhower Doctrine in March 1957. Its purpose was to strengthen friendly governments that faced military threats from the Soviets or Egypt's Nasser. After lobbying by American Jewish leaders, an amendment was added, which guaranteed that the United States would come to Israel's aid if the Jewish state were attacked. Throughout the Sinai crisis, the "shared attitudes of Jewish identification and support for Israel bound together virtually all American Jewish organizations into a potentially strong pressure group."[21]

Relations with the United States also improved. One area of cooperation was in military intelligence. During the Sinai war, Israel had captured large amounts of Soviet-made equipment, which it made available to the United States. Israelis also began to embrace many aspects of American culture, from films to shopping.

In the United States the spirit of Israel was captured in popular films. Ties with biblical Israel were highlighted with the release of such film epics as *The Ten Commandments*, *Moses*, and *David and Bathsheba*. *Cast a Giant Shadow*, the story of Mickey Marcus, a graduate of West Point and a U.S. Army officer who came to Israel in 1948 to forge a Jewish army, highlighted American connections to Israel. The 1960 film of Leon Uris's book *Exodus* was a feat of "great public relations for Israel." These films depicted Jews and Israelis as people with whom "Americans share political ideals, cultural values and religious traditions."

Meanwhile, the influence of the Soviet Union increased in the Middle East, aided in large measure by President Nasser of Egypt. The United States began to appreciate Israel as the only stable pro-Western country in the region. Increased U.S. economic aid followed, as did a greater sensitivity to Israel's unique security needs. But, in spite of the special relationship that developed with the United States, Israel's fears of 1956 returned with a vengeance eleven years later.

1967

The last thing Israelis want is to win wars. We want peace.

—Golda Meir

The 1956 Sinai war provided Israel with important gains: The ability to navigate through the Gulf of Aqaba reversed Egypt's attempt to isolate Israel commercially. The establishment of a United Nations force along the Egyptian border provided Israel with a greater sense of security. The destruction and capture of massive amounts of Soviet-bloc arms during the war severely weakened Egypt, Israel's most strident enemy. And with the help of France, Israel secretly began building a nuclear reactor in Dimona, which would result in Israel joining the exclusive club of nuclear-armed nations.

The war taught Israel that it could not fully depend on others for protection. It also significantly united the American Jewish community in political action. With the White House largely insensitive to their cause, American Jews found members of Congress more receptive and supportive. National Jewish organizations took positions on U.S.

policy toward the Middle East and encouraged their members to contact their elected representatives with their views.

Although the war caused the United States to better understand Israel's security needs, it was not until John F. Kennedy became president in 1961 that relations between both countries materially improved. As a young member of Congress, John F. Kennedy was sympathetic to Israel. In 1947, when the United Nations was considering a solution to the Palestine problem, he addressed a Zionist convention. "It is my conviction," Kennedy said, "that a just solution requires the establishment of a free and democratic Jewish Commonwealth in Palestine . . . so that those members of the people of Israel who desire to work out their destiny under their chosen leaders may do so."[1] In 1951 he became one of the first members of Congress to visit the Jewish state.

During his political quest for the White House, Kennedy befriended Jewish supporters within the Democratic party for whom Israel was an important issue. Speaking to a Jewish audience during the 1960 presidential campaign, Kennedy said, "Friendship for Israel is not a partisan matter; it is a national commitment." To coordinate efforts with the Jewish community, he appointed Myer Feldman, a Washington attorney, as his special counsel with responsibility for Jewish affairs.

When he met Kennedy prior to the election, Israel's David Ben-Gurion was surprised at the candidate's youthfulness. "I couldn't believe," Ben-Gurion later said, "that young boy would be nominated." Jewish votes played a crucial role in Kennedy's narrow victory over Richard Nixon in the 1960 presidential election. At a meeting in New York several months after the election, Kennedy and Ben-Gurion discussed the major problems of the Middle East, including the issue of Arab refugees. During the session, the president surprised Ben-Gurion by taking him aside for a quiet talk. "You know," Kennedy said, "I was elected by the Jews of New York. I will do something for you."[2]

Kennedy was the first president to openly sell arms to Israel. Nevertheless, he maintained friendly relations with the Arab countries and expressed concern about Israel's growing nuclear capabilities. In a 1963 meeting with Shimon Peres, then Israel's deputy defense minister, Kennedy asked about Israel's new nuclear capabilities. Peres, without admitting that Israel was indeed a nuclear power, provided the noncommittal answer that became his country's standard response to such questions. "We will not," Peres said, "introduce nuclear weapons into the region. We will not be the first to do so."[3] On taking office in 1961, Kennedy received a secret report from the Central Intelligence Agency (CIA) on Israel's nuclear capability. "The fact that Israel is working in this field should have come as no surprise," the report stated. "Furthermore, the Soviet-Egyptian project for the construction of a nuclear reactor in Egypt has been known for some time. . . . The Israeli government cannot prudently wait until Egypt produces an atomic weapon before doing something about one of its own."[4] When Kennedy bluntly asked Ben-Gurion about Israel's atomic capacity, the prime minister told him, "We need atomic power for the desalinization of seawater."[5]

President Kennedy acted on Israel's requests for modern arms with which to counteract the growing Arab arsenal. At the same time he tried to influence Middle East leaders to avoid armed conflict. In a personal letter of encouragement to Ben-Gurion, Kennedy wrote: "I would hope that the present quiescence on the borders of Israel will continue undisturbed." Even as the United States joined in a United Nations censure of Israel for a 1961 retaliatory raid on Syria, five batteries of Hawk missiles were on their way to Tel Aviv. Israel, while grateful for the missiles, objected that it was required to pay the full amount in cash.

"We can't [pay in cash]," an Israeli official said. "We don't pay cash for anything. We buy everything on credit." Further investigation revealed that the United States had previously arranged to sell arms to Australia on good credit terms. The president told the secretary of defense, "Let's lend them [Israel] the money on the same terms as the Australians." Myer Feldman recounted that this action "broke the dam," and all future sales of arms to Israel were on equally generous terms.

Ben-Gurion's successor as prime minister, Levi Eshkol, also received assurances from President Kennedy. "The attitude of the United States to the creation of Israel has always been one of sympathy and understanding for your aspiration to reestablish your ancient homeland." The president reiterated America's commitment to Israel while explaining his administration's position of maintaining good relations with all countries in the Middle East. "Our policies and programs in regard to the Arab states have resulted in improved relationships which permit us to talk frankly and realistically to them and enable us to exert some leverage on their action. While I do not wish to overestimate this influence, I am convinced that we can best advance your interests as well as ours by maintaining such relationships and our resultant ability to talk with both sides."[6]

"We have to concern ourselves with the whole Middle East," Kennedy told Foreign Minister Golda Meir during a December 1962 informal meeting at the president's Palm Beach, Florida, home, "[to] maintain our friendship with Israel without constantly cutting across our other interests in the Middle East. If we pulled out of the Arab Middle East and maintained our ties only with Israel this would not be in Israel's interest."[7] Then, to allay Israel's fear of abandonment in the event of another war, Kennedy spoke of the "special United States concern for the security and independence of Israel. We have the will and ability to carry out our stated determination to preserve it."

Mrs. Meir told Kennedy that "Israel welcomes the growing U.S. influence in the Middle East because it will help the Middle East in a way that is friendly to Israel. The Israelis are not a frightened or panicky people, but they are very conscious of their security problems."

Kennedy responded that the "United States is really interested in Israel, as I am personally. We are interested that Israel should keep up its sensitive, tremendous, historic task. What we want from Israel arises because our relationship is a two-way street. Israel's security in the long run depends in part on what it does with the Arabs, but also on us."[8] Mrs. Meir expressed her desire to be able to sit down with Egyptian leaders "for talks which could be held anywhere, just to have direct discussions about our common problems." When Mrs. Meir concluded, the president wanted to reassure his guest. "He took my hand," Mrs. Meir later wrote, "looked into my eyes and said very solemnly, 'I understand, Mrs. Meir, don't worry. Nothing will happen to Israel. . . .'" [9]

The assassination of John F. Kennedy in 1963 emotionally affected America's Jewish community. He had done more to satisfy Israeli security concerns than any of his predecessors. But they had nothing to fear about the continuing relationship. Lyndon Johnson had climbed the political ladder to become majority leader of the United States Senate before he was elected vice president. He always considered himself a friend of Israel. At Kennedy's funeral, Johnson stopped to greet Golda Meir, who stood in a receiving line. He bent down and whispered in her ear, "I know that you have lost a friend but I hope you understand that I, too, am a friend."[10]

In 1964, President Lyndon Johnson welcomed Levi Eshkol to the White House for a kosher dinner to honor the

President John F. Kennedy greets Foreign Minister (later Prime Minister) Golda Meir at the United Nations in 1961. Kennedy's main goal where Israel was concerned was to maintain the delicate balance of relations that existed among the United States, Israel, and the Arab nations.

first official visit of an Israeli prime minister to the United States. (David Ben-Gurion's visits had always been "unofficial.") With the political support of Congress, economic aid to Israel grew, as did the sale of modern weapons, including attack aircraft and tanks previously denied by American administrations. The American Jewish community was not silent on Israel's behalf. "I have rarely been exposed to as much pressure as I have had recently on the question of tanks for Israel," Myer Feldman told President Johnson.

Relative calm had prevailed on Israel's borders in the years immediately following the Suez war of 1956. But gradually, the occasional small-scale incursions increased in size, frequency, and death toll. The legendary CBS News reporter Edward R. Murrow had first visited Israel in 1957 to do a television documentary. When he returned with his wife, Janet, and son, Casey, on a primarily social trip in 1960, his activities were reported in Israeli newspapers. But, ever the reporter, Murrow took the opportunity to visit the Golan Heights with his son to report on the military tension there. Casey later recalled, "One of the officers was showing us where the Syrian gun emplacements were, and I picked up my binoculars and he hit me just like that—really cut me across my nose to get the binoculars out—get the reflection away because he said they'd shoot at that instantly."[11]

Even as tension along Israel's borders increased, the Soviet Union was involving itself more directly in Middle East affairs. Eager to influence the Arab world, the Soviets provided their Arab clients with the latest in arms and encouraged their militant anti-Israel actions to antagonize the United States. With Soviet support, Egypt and Syria agreed in 1963 to federate into a single state to be known as the United Arab Republic. Its stated goal was to liberate "the Arab Nation from the peril of Zionism." Incursions into Israel from Syria in the north, Jordan in the east, and Egypt in the south heightened tensions in the Middle East. The result was a massive eruption of violence in 1967 that dramatically altered the region's balance of power.

A clash on the Syrian border set off the chain of events. On April 7, Syrian troops fired at the driver of a lone unarmored Israeli tractor. An artillery duel with Israel quickly escalated into an air battle during which the Israeli air force shot down six Syrian jet fighters. The Soviets quickly accused Israel of moving large numbers of troops to the Syrian border. In spite of Israel's assurances that the charges were false, a war atmosphere quickly engulfed the region.

On May 16, 1967, Egypt requested the United Nations to immediately withdraw all troops of the UN Emergency Force stationed in northern Sinai and at Sharm al-Sheikh at the gateway to the Gulf of Aqaba. Gamel Abdel Nasser made no pretense about his plans for war. "The battle will be a general one and our basic objective will be to destroy Israel," he declared. "As I have said," Nasser explained, "Israel's existence in itself is an aggression." He also announced that the war would involve troops from other Arab countries. "This is Arab power," he proudly proclaimed. Within two hours of his request, U Thant, the secretary general of the United Nations, announced that the UN troops would indeed withdraw.

The assurances given by the UN, which led Israel to withdraw from captured Sinai and Aqaba in 1956, instantly dissolved. It appeared that Israel would be forced to fight again, only this time against larger, better prepared, and united Arab armies generously provisioned by the Soviet Union.

Tension mounted. By May 20 more than 100,000 well-armed Egyptian soldiers were in the Sinai, facing the border with Israel. Within a week Israel was totally surrounded by a combined Arab force of 250,000 soldiers, 2,000 tanks, and 700 military aircraft. The Israeli government began a quiet mobilization of its own citizen army. On May 22, with the United Nations buffer force gone, Nasser closed the Gulf of Aqaba to Israeli shipping, a blatant act of war. In a radio broadcast to Egyptian troops, Nasser said, "We are in confrontation with Israel. . . . We are ready for war." Israel turned to Britain, France, and the United States for indications of support. Abba Eban was urgently dispatched to London, Paris, and Washington where he forcefully presented Israel's precarious situation. To President Johnson, Eban presented the written assurance that former President Eisenhower had given David Ben-Gurion in 1956 that he [Ben-Gurion] "would never have cause to regret" relying on America's good faith.

In spite of the earlier assurances, the three major powers were reluctant to offer more than moral support. The United States urged both sides to carefully consider their next steps. President Johnson informed Eban that he could not guarantee support for Israel if Israel fired the first shot. "Israel will not be alone unless it decides to go it alone," Johnson told Eban. "I am sure you will understand," the president then wrote, "that I cannot accept any responsibilities on behalf of the United States for situations which arise as the result of actions on which we are not consulted." Eighty-seven members of Congress signed a statement denouncing Nasser and called on President Johnson to support Israel. Johnson issued a statement on May 23 declaring that the United States "considers the Gulf to be an international waterway and feels that a blockade of Israeli shipping is illegal and potentially disastrous to the cause of peace."

When a reporter asked Levi Eshkol if he had expected more tangible aid from the United States, the prime minister responded, "Surely, we expect such help—but we would rely primarily on our own army. I wouldn't want American mothers crying about the blood of their sons being shed here."[12] Defense Minister Shimon Peres was even less optimistic. He told Myer Feldman, "The United States would never come to the defense of Israel. We have to defend ourselves and we know it."[13]

"The army and all the forces are now mobilized," Nasser announced to a frenzied Egyptian populace. "The Jews threatened war. We tell them: You are welcome, we are ready for war." To a military group, Nasser boasted, "There is complete coordination of military action between us and Syria," and he reiterated his basic objective of destroying Israel.

War seemed inevitable. The United States sent the Sixth Fleet into the Mediterranean and assured Israel of its commitment to policies of previous administrations, especially the 1957 promise by President Eisenhower to guarantee Israel's frontiers and the right to freedom of navigation in the Gulf of Aqaba. "You can assure the Israeli Cabinet," Johnson told Eban, "we will pursue vigorously any and all possible measures to keep the Strait open." Privately, administration officials reassured Israelis they "could rely on the President." All that was needed was a single shot.

President Johnson urged Israel to refrain from action for at least two weeks while the United States tried to organize an international flotilla to test Egypt's resolve in the Gulf of Aqaba. Sadly, only two other nations responded to the call of the United States. The Soviet Union continued to inflame the situation and warned the president, "If Israel begins hostilities, the Soviet Union will come to the aid of the attacked countries."[14] Israel agreed to postpone any immediate action. Levi Eshkol later explained, "I did not want to give him [Johnson] a pretext to say later: 'I told you so.'"

But postponement did not mean inaction. Israel quietly mobilized its citizen army and made preparations for war. As thousands of foreign tourists urgently made plans to leave the country, young Israelis filled sandbags and dug air-raid shelters. On May 30, King Hussein of Jordan flew to Cairo and signed a mutual defense pact with Egypt. "The hour of decision has arrived," he warned. So grave was the outlook for survival that, on June 2, Israel's political opposition put aside its differences and joined in a national emergency government coalition with General Moshe Dayan as the new defense minister.

Israelis nervously watched as Kuwaiti and Iraqi forces arrived in Egypt. They listened to radio broadcasts from Arab countries describing the frenzy of street mobs. They heard the threats of the president of Iraq, who told his army officers he would soon meet them in Haifa and Tel Aviv. They heard an Arab officer calmly describe what would happen to Israelis after an Arab victory. "Those who survive," he said, "will remain in Palestine. I estimate that none of them will survive." Hateful speeches and fiery street demonstrations were backed up by a ring of Arab armies, tanks, and planes, which surrounded Israel. Around the world, there was much sympathy and moral support for Israel but little tangible aid.

United States policy toward the Middle East was weak and unfocused. The strong inroads made by the Soviet Union gave the United States only limited influence on the Arab side. All that Secretary of State Dean Rusk could do was restate to Arab leaders that the United States "cannot abandon, in principle, the right of Israeli flag ships to transit the Strait." At the time, President Johnson was preoccupied by an escalating war in Vietnam. Israel, dependent on military aid from the United States, nevertheless, tried to reassure the president that Israel did not expect foreign troops or "anyone else to fight for us."[15]

Israel could not assure the United States, however, that it would not be first to attack. Presidential aide John P. Roche recalled that Johnson "pushed [Eban] for a flat commitment that they would not hit." Eban was noncommittal. "As your friend," President Johnson wrote to Prime Minister Eshkol, "I repeat even more strongly what I said yesterday to Mr. Eban: Israel just must not take preemptive military action and thereby make itself responsible for the initiation of hostilities."[16] Off the record, the president told Roche, "Yes, they're going to hit. There's nothing we can do about it."[17]

Israel felt isolated. Abba Eban later recalled, "Nobody who lived those days in Israel will ever forget the air of heavy foreboding that hovered over our land. . . . For Israel there would be only one defeat."[18] Diplomatic efforts by the United States produced no tangible results. The Soviet Union hardened its attitude, sharply threatening to end "Israeli aggression." Without American support to prevent Soviet military intervention, Israel could not undertake any preemptive strike. The Johnson administration's hard line softened as Secretary of State Dean Rusk told a reporter, "I don't think it is our business to restrain anyone."[19]

With Arab forces massed on Israel's borders poised to attack, war broke out on June 5, 1967. Time was of the essence: Israel's very existence was threatened. In a series of coordinated surprise attacks against Egyptian air bases, Israel virtually destroyed Egypt's air force within hours and assumed complete superiority in the air. Israel sent a message to King Hussein of Jordan urging him to stay out of the war with the promise that Israel "would not initiate any action whatsoever against Jordan." Hussein, however, chose to believe the wishful assurances of Gamal Abdel Nasser that Egyptian troops were already at the outskirts of Tel Aviv and sent Jordanian troops into action.

The State Department press office issued a statement that said: "Our position is neutral in thought, word, and deed." But the United States was far from neutral. President Johnson had promised Abba Eban to politically support the Israeli position. Individual Americans were not neutral, either. A Gallup Poll showed that 55 percent of all Americans sided with Israel; 4 percent with the Arab nations. Nonetheless, American Jews were frightened and gloomy. Images of the Holocaust prevailed throughout the

An Israeli soldier takes aim during the Six-Day War of 1967. Israelis were proud of their country's quick victory, as were Jews worldwide. And unlike the 1956 war, the end of this war did not see a demand by the United States that Israel surrender the lands it had captured.

crisis. Rabbi Abraham Joshua Heschel wrote: "Terror and dread fell upon Jews everywhere. Will God permit our people to perish? Will there be another Auschwitz, another Dachau, another Treblinka?"

"Many Jews would never have believed," Arthur Hertzberg wrote in the August 1967 issue of *Commentary*, a magazine published by the American Jewish Committee, "that grave danger to Israel could dominate their thoughts and emotions to the exclusion of all else." But events in the Middle East instantly transformed most American Jews into active Zionists. By the end of the war, the anti-Zionist American Council for Judaism practically ceased to exist. American Jews raised $240 million in aid for Israel and purchased $190 million worth of Israel Bonds. Ten thousand Americans rushed to Israel to work in agricultural and other noncombat positions as substitutes for hastily mobilized reserve soldiers.

By the fourth day of the war, Israeli troops had advanced to the Suez Canal and were well on their way to recapturing the entire Sinai Peninsula as it had in 1956. An official in Israel's prime minister's office said, "People in the United States, Britain and France have forgotten 1956 but we haven't. The memory haunts us. We won the Sinai campaign with guns and lost it with words." Egyptian forces were totally shattered. Four hundred of their tanks were destroyed and two hundred more captured. Ten thousand Egyptian soldiers were dead and another twelve thousand taken prisoner. With the destruction of the Egyptian army, Israel turned its attention to Jordan and Syria. In fierce fighting, Israel gained control of much of the West Bank of the Jordan River, including the important cities of Bethlehem and Jericho. Attention turned to the Jordanian-held part of Jerusalem. Because holy sites revered by Christians, Muslims, and Jews were involved, heavy artillery could not be used. Instead, street by street infantry action—with heavy casualties on both sides—maintained the safety of the holy places.

On June 7, Israeli paratroopers entered the Old City of Jerusalem through the Lion's Gate and reclaimed the Western Wall, which had been under Jordanian rule since 1948. Since that time all Jews had been forbidden to visit this holiest of sites. The first dust-covered Israeli soldiers who reached the Wall gently touched the stones, prayed, and wept. Defense Minister Moshe Dayan stated, "We have unified Jerusalem, the divided capital of Israel. We have returned to the holiest of our holy places never to depart from it again."

In the north, Israeli troops gained control of the Golan Heights, from whose fortified villages Syria had been able to shell Israeli settlements at will. By the tenth of June, Israeli armor was on the road to Damascus, Syria's capital.

Jews around the world, including those in the United States, felt a new pride in their religion and their connections to Israel. Many felt they were experiencing a religious miracle. In six days the tiny Jewish state had managed to defeat the combined armies of five heavily armed Arab nations and add a huge chunk of territory to its new map of the region. Israel was in possession of the entire Sinai Peninsula right up to the east bank of the Suez Canal, the Gaza Strip, the Golan Heights, and the West Bank of the Jordan River, including the unified city of Jerusalem. A United Nations cease-fire brought the war to an end on June 11. Nasser could not believe the extent of his defeat and falsely accused the United States of fighting for Israel. "The enemy was operating an air force three times its normal strength," the incredulous Egyptian leader complained.

"I have never concealed my regret," President Johnson later wrote, "that Israel decided to move when it did." Nevertheless, unlike the aftermath of the 1956 war, the United States did not demand Israeli surrender of captured land. President Johnson spoke on June 19, 1967, about a negotiated solution to the Arab-Israeli conflict. "There must also be recognized rights of national life," he said, "progress in solving the refugee problem, freedom of maritime passage, limitation of the arms race, and respect for political independence and territorial integrity." Abba Eban stated, "There can be no substitute for a directly negotiated peace settlement." When the head of the Jewish War Veterans visited the White House in August 1967, the president told him that the United States would "stand firm behind its program for a Middle East settlement."

Israel was not the only winner in the Six-Day War, as it came to be known. When the fighting ended, Israel found itself in possession of vast quantities of the latest Soviet military equipment. As a sign of appreciation, Israel allowed U.S. intelligence agencies free access to the most secret of the Cold War enemy's arms technology.

There was one major incident during this time, which dampened American relations with Israel. On June 8, 1967, Israeli war planes had attacked the USS *Liberty*, an American intelligence-gathering ship, mistaking it for an Egyptian vessel. At the time, the *Liberty* was steaming slowly off the Gaza Strip, intercepting the radio messages of the combatants. Before the error was discovered, thirty-four Americans were dead and seventy-five injured. Israel apologized and paid more than $100 million in compensation to the victims and their families.

Continued American support for Israel took many forms. When the war was over, Israel requested fifty F-4 Phantom jet fighters from the United States. To counteract State Department opposition, Jewish groups led by the American Israel Public Affairs Committee (AIPAC) began a concerted lobbying effort on Congress. The result was a Sense of Congress resolution calling on President Johnson to quickly conclude the sale of the Phantoms to Israel. At a summit conference held soon after the war's end at Glassboro State College in New Jersey, Soviet Premier Aleksei Kosygin asked President Johnson why the United States was so supportive of Israel. The president of the United States answered, "Because it is right."

Ephraim (Eppie) Evron, an Israeli diplomat in Washington, was a friend and confidant of President Johnson. Speaking to American Jewish groups after the 1967 war, Evron told his listeners, "I have the strongest interest in the

United States helping Israel and I can tell you that Lyndon Johnson saved Israel."

Shortly after the war, Israel proposed to negotiate with the Arab states and return nearly all of the captured land in return for a guarantee of true peace. Arab leaders gathered at a conference in Khartoum, Sudan in August 1967 and roundly rejected the offer. This decision formed the basis of Arab policy toward Israel for the next two decades: no peace with Israel, no recognition of Israel, and no negotiation with Israel.

1973

Mrs. Meir, nothing will happen to Israel. We are committed to you.

—John F. Kennedy

Mr. President, I believe you one hundred percent. I just want to be sure we're still there by the time you honor your commitment.

—Golda Meir

The 1967 war marked a turning point in the history of modern Israel. Since its birth in 1948, the young country had experienced a seemingly endless series of wars, incursions, and infiltrations by its Arab neighbors. The image of a beleaguered nation maintaining itself against all odds captured the sympathy of many around the world. With the decisive end of the Six-Day War in Israel's favor, the position of underdog shifted to the Arabs and altered the balance of power between Israel and its neighbors.

Israel's new feeling of self-confidence was checked by the reality of a new type of war, which emerged after 1967.

In place of defined battlefields and military strategy, violence against Israeli civilians and military took the form of nearly continuous guerrilla attacks from across the borders. Israel, the unrivaled victor of one of the fastest wars on record, assumed a defensive posture. In the five-month period from March to July 1969, sixty-one Israelis were killed and hundreds more wounded.

Richard M. Nixon was the Republican candidate for president of the United States in 1968. Jewish Americans had supported the Democratic party for decades, and the year 1968 was no different. Eighty-one percent of American Jews voted for Hubert Humphrey, even though Nixon had made pro-Israel speeches during the campaign. "Israel," he said, "must possess sufficient military power to deter an attack. Sufficient power means the balance must be tipped in Israel's favor." Most Jewish voters were not convinced. "We assumed," Abba Eban explained, "that he would continue Dwight Eisenhower's reserved attitude to Israel."[1]

The Middle East quickly became a foreign policy concern for the new Nixon administration. Shortly after the election, Nixon sent former Pennsylvania governor William Scranton on a fact-finding trip to the region. Scranton promised the Arab countries that the new president was prepared to pursue an "evenhanded" policy in the region. To Israel, sensitive to even the smallest change of American attitude, that meant a time of diplomatic unease.

In 1969, Secretary of State William Rogers developed that "balanced" plan. The Rogers Plan called for Israel to withdraw from nearly all territory gained during the Six-Day War, take back all refugees, and agree to the internationalization of Jerusalem in exchange for a binding peace treaty arrived at through direct Arab-Israeli negotiations. Israel rejected the plan at once: It needed more tangible assurances from its neighbors. "Israel won't accept this," said Golda Meir, who became prime minister that year.

"We're not going to commit suicide." In January 1970 more than 1,400 American Jewish leaders arrived in Washington to protest the Rogers Plan. AIPAC, the American Israel Public Affairs Committee, arranged appointments for the visitors with 250 members of Congress. The lobbying effort did not hurt their cause. But in the end the Rogers Plan derailed when the Arabs also rejected it: They were unwilling to even talk with the Jewish state.

The Soviet Union took advantage of the situation to rearm Egypt and Syria and encourage a war of attrition against Israel. This new "war" featured indiscriminate artillery attacks across the Suez Canal and "hit and run" raids by guerrilla bands on military and civilian targets. The goal was to damage Israel's economy, lower morale, and force a return of captured land without Arab concessions or recognition of Israel. The attacks across the Suez did lessen in the summer of 1970 when Israel and Egypt finally agreed to a cease-fire, but not before there were heavy casualties on both sides.

Not satisfied with the continued failure of the Arab nations to defeat Israel, the Palestinians decided to take action on their own. The Palestine Liberation Organization (PLO) had been established in 1964 as a confederation of various Palestinian groups dedicated to the elimination of Israel. Under the leadership of Yasir Arafat, the PLO engaged in diplomatic and guerrilla activity against the Jewish state. Arafat was one of the founders of Fatah, a Palestinian group dedicated to armed struggle against Israel. Throughout the 1970s and 1980s, PLO-affiliated groups carried out acts of terrorism including airline hijackings, the massacre of Israeli athletes at the 1972 Olympics at Munich, Germany, and attacks on civilians inside Israel.

In 1974 the PLO was recognized by the Arab nations as the "sole, legitimate representative of the Palestinian people." As the PLO sought diplomatic recognition, Israel and the United States worked at denying it such recognition from international organizations. The policy of the United States was to not recognize or even speak with the PLO until that organization renounced the use of terrorism and recognized the right of Israel to exist. To soften its image, the PLO amended its charter to favor "a democratic, secular state in all of Palestine" instead of "driving the Jews into the sea." The change sounded better, but the goal was still the demise of the Jewish state.

Hijackings of civilian aircraft by Arab terrorist groups attracted world attention and only hardened Israel's resolve to assure its own security. Israel's usual practice was to respond to terrorist acts with reprisal raids against Palestinian targets. Israel tried turning to the United Nations for help, but the international organization was not sympathetic to Israel's complaints.

Nonetheless, Israel did not hesitate to retaliate against Arab attacks. On December 28, 1968, an Israeli task force, reacting to recent Arab skyjacking attempts, landed at the Beirut, Lebanon, airport and destroyed thirteen civilian aircraft on the ground. This time, to Israel's dismay, even the United States joined in a United Nations Security Council condemnation of Israel.

In response to Egyptian bombardments across the Suez Canal in March 1969, Israeli artillery targeted Egyptian oil installations, causing enormous damage. The Soviets, ignoring the fact that this was retaliation and not outright aggression, stated in a Radio Moscow broadcast, "It appears that the extremists in Israel intend to continue increasing tension in the Near East." On July 21, Israel sent another "message" in response to continuing Egyptian commando raids with an air attack, which destroyed fortifications and Soviet radar installations on Egypt's Green Island. Israel's air force overrode Egyptian radar and conducted air raids deep into Egyptian territory. The "message" was not received. In a speech on July 23, Nasser said, "The Six-Day War is not over . . . we have not yet entered the full extent of the military struggle—that is still ahead of us."

Golda Meir ignored the heated speeches, which continued at the United Nations, but still hoped for a way to end the cycle of violence with Israel's neighbors. "The death of one of our boys," she said, "causes us more grief than the death of one hundred Egyptians causes Nasser, judging from his actions. . . . We must sit down and solve our problems together."

In September 1969, Golda Meir flew to Washington for a face-to-face meeting with President Nixon. She came not only to request long-range military and economic help but to convince the president of Israel's need for security. The president welcomed the Israeli prime minister to the White House with great public flourish but with careful words. "We are neither pro-Arab nor pro-Israel," he said. "We are pro peace." Privately, he told her that in spite of the Rogers Plan he sympathized with Israel's desire to achieve peace "through a freely negotiated agreement between the parties of the contract." When American Jews questioned Golda Meir's support of Nixon she responded, "Have you any liberals who can supply us with Phantoms?"[2] Phantom jets were indeed promised by President Nixon, but delivery occurred only months later as a direct result of a strategic favor by Israel to the United States.

Fighting in the Middle East was not always exclusively targeted at Israel during that time. In 1970, Syria invaded Jordan, hoping to overthrow King Hussein with the help of refugee Palestinians, who made up a majority of Jordan's population. The Palestinians were angry because the king had put pressure on their guerrillas to curtail their raids on Israel from Jordanian soil. The United States did not want to involve American troops in the defense of Jordan and thereby give the Soviets an excuse to intervene. At the same time, the United States needed to keep Soviet-backed Syria from overrunning Jordan. In a reversal of roles, Israel came

President Richard Nixon's support of Israel was tempered
by his desire to keep U.S. relations balanced in the Middle
East. Prime Minister Meir defended her support of Nixon
to critics, however, because he did eventually provide
Israel with Phantom jets.

to America's aid by massing its own troops on the Golan Heights. Simultaneously, Nixon placed 20,000 American troops on alert and reinforced the American naval presence in the Mediterranean. The Syrians took the hint and withdrew. A grateful Nixon Administration quickly sent Israel the Phantom jets and Skyhawk bombers promised months earlier.

More importantly, the event marked the beginning of a meaningful strategic relationship between the United States and Israel. Sometimes rocky, the relationship was nurtured by President Nixon's secretary of state, Dr. Henry Kissinger. The son of German Jewish parents who had escaped the Holocaust, Kissinger was a brilliant Harvard University professor. As head of the president's National Security Council, he encouraged Nixon to break the Cold War impasse between the United States and the Communist nations. They both also believed that the interests of the United States would be aided by a final resolution of the Arab-Israeli conflict. The Soviets were not cooperative. While they continued to funnel increasing amounts of arms to Egypt and Syria, they made no efforts to curtail the Arab war of attrition against Israel and used every opportunity to lay blame for the conflict exclusively on Israel.

Nixon and Kissinger believed the Soviet Union was behind the Syrian adventure into Jordan. In reaction, Nixon's public support of Israel increased. Speaking to a gathering of the United Jewish Appeal, Israeli Defense Minister Moshe Dayan praised Nixon, perhaps a bit too generously. "He kept every word he told us since he came to power."

In spite of praise-filled speeches, Israel's concerns about the slow arms flow from the United States continued. Leaders such as Golda Meir visited Washington on a regular basis. "The other side has a constant flow of arms," Meir said in 1970. "Is it too much to ask from the United States that the supply of arms needed for our defense be based on an ongoing relationship, without the necessity for us to negotiate each time for additional shipments?"[3] Earlier that year, seventy-nine U.S. senators had signed a letter to Secretary of State Rogers urging the immediate supply of aircraft to Israel.

On September 28, 1970, Gamal Abdel Nasser died of a heart attack at age fifty-two. He was succeeded by Anwar Sadat, who began to systematically reverse the Socialist political and economic course set by Nasser. In 1972, Sadat expelled Soviet advisers from Egypt as a result of differences involving strategies. Sadat also tried to build a peace effort with Israel based on the cease-fire agreement, which had ended the war of attrition along the Suez Canal. When initial negotiations could not produce results, however, Sadat began planning a new war against Israel.

Israel, meanwhile, was besieged by increased acts of terrorism. In May a group of Japanese posing as tourists walked off an Air France plane at Israel's Lod Airport, pulled out automatic weapons, and began firing indiscriminately. Twelve people died and fifty were wounded. In September a horrified world looked on as eleven Israeli athletes participating in the Olympic Games at Munich, Germany, were taken hostage and murdered.

World sympathy for Israel did not extend to the United Nations, however, which took no action on either tragedy. And then, as if to underline its attitude, the United Nations—with the United States abstaining—adopted a resolution calling on all member states not to recognize any Israeli actions in occupied territory. The diplomatic and terrorist actions did nothing to weaken Israel's resolve not to leave occupied territory without a comprehensive peace with the Arabs.

Richard Nixon was reelected president in a 1972 landslide. He garnered nearly 40 percent of the Jewish vote; up from a mere 17 percent just four years earlier. American Jews now perceived him as a friend and supporter of Israel. After a March 1973 meeting in Washington with Nixon,

Golda Meir told reporters she had "no regrets about this visit. I can say," she continued, "that we have a good friend at the White House."

The relative calm of the cease-fire period between Israel and Egypt begun in 1970 was shattered at 2:00 P.M., October 6, 1973, on Yom Kippur, the holiest day of the Jewish year. Those at prayer in synagogues throughout Israel began to notice people whispering as individuals put aside their prayer books, kissed loved ones, and left. Radio stations, always stilled for the solemn day, began broadcasting coded messages. It did not take long for the entire country to know that in coordinated surprise attacks, Egyptian troops had crossed the Suez Canal as Syrian forces invaded the Golan Heights.

Israeli intelligence had earlier evaluated reconnaissance photos of the Arab military buildup but concluded that there was "little likelihood of war." American intelligence sources insisted that the Arab buildup was "defensive in nature" and did not indicate an "imminent military action." Nonetheless, Israeli leaders were nervous. Unlike in 1967, when Israel reacted to the Arab military buildup, Israel was constrained by its reliance on U.S. support. "America's ability to help Israel," Henry Kissinger had said, "would be impaired if Israel struck first." More bluntly, Kissinger warned Israeli Ambassador Simcha Dinitz, "Don't ever start the war. Don't even preempt! If you fire the first shot, you won't have a dogcatcher in this country supporting you. You won't have presidential support. You'll be all alone. We wouldn't be able to help you. Don't preempt it."

A reluctant Golda Meir agreed. She later recalled, "We could have talked till our faces turned blue and no one would have believed that Israel had acted in self-defense." She feared that by striking first, Israel would be left without any friends in the international community. As Israel waited for the certain attack, Moshe Dayan confidently

Although Israel was aware of an Arab military buildup in the fall of 1973, the United States had issued a stern warning to the Israelis not to strike first, as they had done in 1967. Instead, Egyptian and Syrian forces struck Israel simultaneously on Yom Kippur, the holiest day of the Jewish year. Here, enemy planes bomb an Israeli convoy as soldiers move for cover.

said, "Six years ago we couldn't have taken such risks [to absorb a first blow], but after all, Sinai is far away and we can allow ourselves such a tactic or strategy."[4]

The Yom Kippur attack may not have been a complete surprise to the Israelis, but it certainly was a shock. The Egyptians had prepared well. They launched sophisticated landings across the Canal and overran Israel's vaunted Bar-Lev line of reinforced communication bunkers, command posts, and artillery positions. Both Egypt and Syria were armed with the latest in Soviet surface-to-air missiles, which effectively neutralized Israel's air force. This would not be a repeat of the 1967 war. Israel found itself fighting trained Arab soldiers and began to run out of essential ammunition, fuel, and replacement parts. Israel needed help.

In Washington, President Nixon had his own problems. Vice President Spiro Agnew was about to resign because of corruption charges, and the president was getting more deeply enmeshed in the Watergate scandal that would eventually lead to his resignation. The president relied increasingly on National Security Council head Henry Kissinger. In August a preoccupied Nixon also appointed Kissinger as secretary of state, giving him total responsibility for U.S. foreign policy.

The first days of the new war went badly for Israel. Casualties were high and strategies lacking. In spite of Israel's plea for military aid, the United States was slow in responding. Some experts blamed Kissinger. The new secretary of state assumed that Israel would eventually win, but he did not want to see a rerun of the 1967 war. "The strategy was to prevent Israel from humiliating Egypt again," Kissinger later said. "From the beginning," he explained, "I was determined to use the war to start a peace process." The calculated U.S. policy sought to prevent Israel from achieving a total victory and keep the Soviet Union from intervening on the Arab side.

In the first forty hours of the war Israel lost more than forty planes and two hundred tanks. News of hundreds of Israeli casualties drove home the message that the war was not going well. On October 7, Israel requested an urgent and massive resupply of arms from the United States. Still thinking that Israel would ultimately win, the Nixon administration ignored the plea for help. "We don't want to be so pro-Israel," Nixon told Kissinger, "that the oil states—the Arabs not involved in the fighting—will break ranks and join in the war." Kissinger noted, "The Arab world would be inflamed against us." But by October 9 the United

States was finally convinced that Israel really was in trouble. On October 10 the Israelis were forced from the Bar-Lev fortifications along the Suez Canal. When a member of Congress asked the president, "Is Israel going to lose?" Nixon answered, "No, we will not let Israel go down the tubes." President Nixon ordered Kissinger to inform Israel that the United States would replace all its losses. Meanwhile, massive Soviet airlifts brought fresh arms and ammunition into Egypt and Syria daily.

The American Jewish community sprang into action at news of the war. Like the Israeli and American governments, the Jewish community had an exaggerated view of Israel's military strength as a legacy of the Six-Day War. But their initial confidence was quickly shattered. By the evening of October 6, fund-raising and lobbying efforts were under way. The United Jewish Appeal, Israel Bonds, the Israel Emergency Fund, and other organizations began canvassing Jewish and non-Jewish supporters of Israel. In the first week of the war, more than $100 million was raised. Support came from Fundamentalist Christian groups and labor unions, as well as traditional Jewish sources. "It's a spontaneous uprising," one UJA staff person said. Mass rallies were organized in New York and Washington calling for American aid for Israel. Newspaper editorials and members of Congress lent their important voices to the cause. Henry Kissinger kept reassuring the Israelis that help was on the way. Nevertheless, in Israel, a sense of abandonment prevailed. Golda Meir kept asking, "Where is the airlift?"

Ambassador Simcha Dinitz was in constant contact with the secretary of state, but losing patience with each successive conversation. On October 12, Dinitz told Kissinger that "Israel is running out of ammunition." The secretary of state again promised that American aid was forthcoming. But the administration was bogged down in a dispute about how to fly materials to Israel. Dinitz warned Kissinger that unless aid was sent immediately he would publicly approach Congress.

Meanwhile, Golda Meir appealed to Nixon. "You know the reasons why we took no preemptive action," she wrote. "Our failure to take such action is the reason for our situation now." Foreign Minister Eban flew to Washington and accompanied Ambassador Dinitz on an October 12 meeting with Kissinger. This time, the secretary assured them that American transport planes were indeed scheduled to begin flying to Israel the following day.

At the White House, President Nixon began to fear that without immediate aid, the possibility existed that a desperate Israel might resort to its secret cache of nuclear weapons. The massive Soviet airlift of arms to the Arabs also induced the president to act. On October 13 the president finally cut through the bureaucratic delays and issued a clear order, "Get them in the air, now!" Later that day the first thirty Air Force C-130 transport planes were on their way to Israel.

Once the airlift began, huge military transports landed in the Azores, islands off the coast of Portugal in the Atlantic, every 15 minutes for refueling. The Azores had to be used because America's allies refused permission for the planes to use the more convenient European NATO bases for fear of Arab oil embargoes against Europe. During the next week, 550 American missions landed around the clock in Israel with desperately needed military supplies, including tanks and Phantom jet fighters. Golda Meir watched as the first plane touched down. Tears of gratitude rolled down her cheeks. The airlift, she later said, "not only lifted our spirits, but also served to make the American position clear to the Soviet Union, and it undoubtedly served to make our victory possible."[5] Many Israeli leaders felt they could not have survived without the massive American aid. "Thank God I was right to reject the idea of preemptive strike," Meir said. "It might have saved lives in the beginning, but I am sure that we would not have had that airlift, which is now saving as many lives."[6]

In the north, Israeli forces cleared the Syrians out of the Golan Heights. In the south, Israeli air attacks deep inside Egypt paved the way for cross Canal raids. After an initial setback on the ground, Israeli troops were on the offensive. Massive tank battles took place on the Golan Heights and in the Suez Canal area.

When Soviet cargo planes landed in Damascus, Syria, with more than twenty tons of military supplies, it signaled that the Soviets were prepared to intervene to avoid a new Arab defeat. Kissinger warned Soviet ambassador Anatoly Dobrynin that "any Soviet military intervention would be met by American force." On October 15, Soviet Premier Aleksei Kosygin arrived in Cairo. Publicly, he declared that the Soviet Union "aimed at helping the peoples of the Arab countries liberate their lands seized by Israel."[7] Privately, he urged Sadat to accept a cease-fire, a situation Egypt had previously spurned.

As Israeli troops in the north continued their advance toward Damascus, the Soviets warned Israel to withdraw. At the same time the Soviets approached the United States with a proposal that the combatants immediately accept a cease-fire. In many ways that proposal fit President Nixon's desire for "a battlefield stalemate" so that each side would consider itself a winner and bring everyone to the conference table as equals. When the Soviets expressed concern about the influence of American Jewish voters, Nixon assured Soviet leader Leonid Brezhnev, "United States political considerations will have absolutely no, repeat, no, influence on our decisions. . . . I am prepared to pressure the Israelis to the extent required."[8]

This tough stand was designed to influence the Soviets. "Under no circumstances," Nixon later wrote in his memoirs, "were we going to allow a Soviet airlift to Israel's enemies to lead to an Israeli defeat. Strategic considerations were crucial. The airlift was important as a measure of United States reliability." Sixty-seven U.S. senators informed the president that they strongly supported America sending whatever military supplies, including Phantom jets, needed by Israel to "repel the aggressors." On October 19, President Nixon asked Congress for $2.2 billion in emergency aid for Israel. It was a strong signal to the Soviets and the Arabs that the United States would not let Soviet airlifts of supplies to Egypt and Syria upset the military balance in the Middle East.

As Israel's troops began encircling Egypt's Third Army in the Sinai, Sadat told the Soviets they were ready to accept a cease-fire in place. Not willing to accept any Israeli victory, the Soviets turned to the United States and demanded not only the cease-fire, but a total Israeli pull back to the pre-1967 borders. The Soviets invited Secretary of State Kissinger to Moscow to discuss details. Kissinger readily agreed. "It would keep the issue out of the United Nations," he later said, "until we had shaped an acceptable outcome. . . . It would gain at least another seventy-two hours for military pressures to build."[9]

The delay allowed Israel to improve its position and totally encircle the 25,000 soldiers of Egypt's Third Army. At the same time other Israeli units advanced to within 50 miles (80 kilometers) of Cairo. As Kissinger flew to Moscow he learned that Saudi Arabia had begun an oil embargo against the United States. Long gas-station lines, shortened tempers, and a national fuel emergency tested the patience and resolve of all Americans.

On October 22 the United Nations Security Council adopted Resolution 338—based on the results of discussions between the United States and the Soviet Union—which required both sides in the conflict to accept a cease-fire within twelve hours and begin negotiations toward implementation of previous UN Resolution 242. Great pressure was exerted on Israel to accept the cease-fire even as Israel wanted more time to totally destroy the Egyptian Third Army. While Kissinger was pleased with Israel's advances, he also did not want Egypt to be humiliated and thereby miss an opportunity to have both sides begin meaningful peace talks. Thus began Secretary of State Henry Kissinger's famed "shuttle diplomacy"—constantly flying from one side to the other—which ultimately led to the war's end. Kissinger strongly believed that face-to-face negotiations could accomplish what formal meetings could not.

The cease-fire went into effect on October 23. Israel accepted it only after Golda Meir received a personal message from President Nixon. "We had no choice," one Israeli official said. "We were hardly in a position to say no." Mrs. Meir later wrote: "There is nothing to be ashamed of when a small country like Israel has to give in sometimes to the United States."[10]

Still, sporadic shooting continued as the Egyptian Third Army found itself cut off from its supply links—it had no food, water, or medical aid. Speaking to the Knesset, Israel's parliament, Mrs. Meir said that Israel would not withdraw from any position before negotiations. The Soviets demanded that the United States exert influence over Israel. "If you find it impossible to act jointly with us in this matter," Soviet leader Leonid Brezhnev wrote Nixon, "we should be faced with the necessity to urgently consider the question of taking appropriate steps unilaterally." With the Soviet threat to send military forces to free the surrounded Third Army, President Nixon ordered a worldwide military and nuclear "precautionary alert."

The brief superpower scare was defused on October 27 when the United Nations Security Council organized a peacekeeping force of soldiers from smaller nations to act as a buffer between Israelis and Arabs. Meanwhile, Henry Kissinger urged Israel to allow needed supplies to reach the desperate soldiers of Egypt's Third Army. "No matter how," Kissinger later wrote, "the Third Army had to be saved from its plight."[11]

On November 1, Golda Meir traveled to Washington to personally thank President Nixon. Nixon assured her that "the security and well-being of Israel" was a major U.S. concern. A few days earlier, at a leadership meeting of the American Jewish Committee, members praised President Nixon and Secretary Kissinger "for their refusal to buckle under Soviet pressure. . . ."

During the war, 2,700 Israelis died and 6,000 were wounded—a huge number considering Israel's small population. More than 100 military aircraft were destroyed, as was one third of all Israel's tanks. President Nixon assured Israel that the United States would replace all the material losses. On November 11, at Kilometer 101 on the Cairo-Suez Road, Israel and Egypt formally signed a truce ending the hostilities. The long-suffering Egyptian Third Army was finally freed.

The war fundamentally changed once again the balance of power in the Middle East. Both sides realized there had to be a move toward settlement. Secretary Kissinger embarked on a new series of eleven exhausting "shuttle trips" between Israel, Egypt, and Syria. The results were three specific interim disengagement agreements to separate the armies. In the first, which became known as Sinai I, in January 1974, Egypt and Israel agreed to a limited disengagement. Israel agreed to withdraw 9 to 12 miles (15 to 20 kilometers) to allow for a United Nations buffer zone with Egypt. The second agreement allowed for Israel's complete withdrawal from the west bank of the Suez Canal. The third agreement allowed Israel and Syria to disengage on the Golan Heights.

Israel was in political turmoil after the Yom Kippur War amid charges that the country had not been prepared. In April 1974, Golda Meir resigned as prime minister. As peace gradually returned to the region, terrorism against Israeli targets by Palestinians resumed. That month, eighteen people, mostly women and children, were killed by terrorists in the Israeli immigrant town of Kiryat Shimona, close to the Lebanese border. On May 15, one hundred children were taken hostage in their school in the northern town of Maalot. In the rescue attempt, twenty children were killed; sixty-three were wounded. Other attacks on Israeli civilian targets outraged many in and out of the country.

In June 1974, Richard Nixon, besieged by the Watergate scandal at home, became the first American president to visit Israel. In spite of the difficulties in arranging the massive airlift of military supplies during the recent war, Nixon was welcomed as a hero on his last foreign trip before resigning from the presidency. Waving American flags, 100,000 cheering Israelis lined the route to Jerusalem's King David Hotel. Children chanted, "Nixon! Nixon!" At a gala dinner at the Knesset, Nixon spoke heartfelt words of advice to the new Israeli government led by Yitzhak Rabin. "It also takes courage," Nixon said after praising the success of Israel's army, "a different kind of courage, to wage peace. . . . War is not a solution for Israel's survival, and, above all, it is not right. . . ."

Richard Nixon resigned on August 9, 1974. He was succeeded by Vice President Gerald R. Ford, the former minority leader of the House of Representatives, selected by Nixon to fill out the vice-presidential term of Spiro Agnew. As a member of Congress, Ford was known as a friend of Israel and had often voted to aid the Jewish state and support Jewish causes.

In September 1974, Israeli Prime Minister Yitzhak Rabin made an official visit to the United States. Relations between the United States and Israel had cooled over Israel's refusal to accept peace in the Middle East at any cost. The United States wanted Israel to make concessions to the Arabs with the hope of peace to come. Israelis were not willing to withdraw from occupied territory without formal peace agreements with its neighbors. To avoid misunderstanding, Henry Kissinger advised Ford to tell Rabin that their meeting was not "a confrontation but a meeting among friends to devise a strategy for peace."[12]

At a meeting with the president in December, Jewish leaders expressed concern about the worldwide pressure upon Israel to unilaterally give up territory. President Ford said, "As long as I am President, there will be no Munich in the Middle East," referring to Hitler's unopposed annexation of a chunk of Czechoslovakia just prior to the outbreak of World War II. Ford also told the gathering that the United States sought to follow a step-by-step procedure to involve all parties in the Middle East in a peace process.

They were also gravely concerned about perceived anti-Semitism at the United Nations. In November, dominated by Arab and Communist delegations, the United Nations Educational, Scientific and Cultural Organization (UNESCO) voted to exclude Israel. In response, the U.S. Congress stopped payment of American dues to UNESCO. On December 9, seventy-one members of the U.S. Senate wrote President Ford to "reaffirm the commitment to the survival and integrity of the State of Israel that has been the bipartisan basis of American policy over twenty-six years and under five administrations." Continuing the allusion Ford had made to Munich, the senators added, "We do not believe that a policy of appeasement will be any more successful now than it proved to be in Europe in the 1930s. . . ."

Henry Kissinger continued his "shuttle diplomacy" between Egypt and Israel. He met resistance from Israel, which was nervous about President Sadat's reluctance to make a formal declaration of nonbelligerency against Israel and publicly make peace. Kissinger's mission concluded without an agreement that could bring Israel to the negotiation table. President Ford felt that in spite of the fact that the Nixon administration had supplied Israel with arms at a greater rate than previous administrations, Israeli leaders were misleading Ford and Kissinger by allowing the shuttle diplomacy to continue without any sign of agreement. In anger, he wrote a letter to Prime Minister Rabin. "Failure of the negotiations," Ford said, "will have a far-reaching impact on the region and on our relations. I have given instructions for a reassessment of our relations with Israel." With that warning, President Ford, long considered a friend of Israel, suspended negotiations on Israel's request for additional F-15 fighter planes and Lance missiles. He hoped that the shock of his actions would force Israel to reconsider and withdraw from captured territory even without a formal peace agreement with Egypt. "Our reassessment," Ford later wrote, "jolted the American Jewish community and Israel's many friends in Congress. . . . I knew that I would come under intense pressure soon to change our policy, but I was determined to hold firm."

More than seven hundred leaders of the American Jewish community gathered in New York to discuss the reassessment. Full-page ads on Israel's behalf were taken out in leading newspapers, and a serious lobbying effort on Congress began by AIPAC. In May, seventy-six members of the U.S. Senate wrote the president urging the administration to submit a foreign-aid request to Congress that "will be responsive to Israel's urgent military and economic needs." All sides knew that Israel was dependent upon the United States diplomatically and economically. Since the Yom Kippur War, the United States had given Israel more than $3 billion in aid, including one hundred F-4 and A-4 fighter airplanes, seven hundred tanks, and ammunition. Israel's army was stronger than it had been in 1973. A "reassessment" could be harmful to Israel.

In a letter, Rabbi Israel Miller, the chairman of the Conference of Presidents of Major American Jewish Organizations, told President Ford of the Jewish community's concern about the reassessment and the continuation of

President Truman had his Eddie Jacobson, and President Gerald Ford (left) had his Max Fisher. Fisher (right) had been a fund-raiser for the Republican party and a trusted confidant to President Richard Nixon. He continued his unofficial role as adviser on Jewish affairs in the Ford administration, working with the president very closely to maintain U.S.-Israeli relations in a tense period of history.

American aid to Israel. "America's greatest contribution to the cause of its own security and of peace in the Middle East," he concluded, "lies not in any imposed 'solution' nor in pressure or threat. It lies in making clear our country's enduring commitment to the security of Israel."

President Ford needed a way to improve relations with the Jewish community. Enter Max Fisher. Like Eddie Jacobson during the Truman years, Fisher served President Ford as an unofficial liaison to Jewish community leaders.

Fisher was a self-made millionaire and philanthropist active in Jewish community affairs who met frequently with Israeli leaders. As a fund-raiser for the Republican party, Fisher had become a trusted confidant to President Nixon and unofficial adviser on Jewish affairs. Fisher continued this role into succeeding Republican administrations, particularly the administration of Gerald Ford, who, like Fisher, came from Michigan. Fisher was one of a select few who had instant access to the Oval Office and met often with the president on Jewish issues.

In early April, Fisher traveled to Israel, ostensibly on Jewish Agency business. In three separate secret meetings totaling five hours, Fisher talked with Israeli Prime Minister Yitzhak Rabin about the worsening diplomatic relations with the Ford administration. In their concluding meeting, Rabin told Fisher, "Max, tell Kissinger and Ford not to worry—the process will continue. The talks will be resumed. But there is no need to rush." On his return to Washington, Fisher went to the White House to meet with Ford and Kissinger on April 9. Reading from a nine-page report he had written during the night with the help of former Ford aide Leonard Garment, Fisher told the president, "One cannot overemphasize the Israelis' preoccupation with the question of physical security." Garment later said that meeting was "one of the most important meetings in the history of American-Israeli relations."[13] "They [Israelis] do not take the friendship of America lightly," Fisher continued, "and suffer through any decision that threatens the strength of that friendship."[14]

Fisher suggested a "cooling off" period to "clear the air." He told Ford, "New strengths and new opportunities exist now that did not exist before, and these are the direct result of the recent negotiations that you and the Secretary set in motion." Finally, Fisher recommended that Ford "narrow the scope of your planned 'reassessment' of Middle East policy. This should be done in your address to the Congress tomorrow." Ford was convinced. The next day, President Gerald Ford delivered a scheduled "State of the World" televised address to a joint session of Congress. Without once using the word "reassessment," Ford said, "The issues dividing [Israel and Egypt] are vital to them and not amenable to easy and quick solutions." The next morning a front-page newspaper photo showed an otherwise unidentified Max Fisher sitting prominently with the Ford family in the visitors' gallery of the House of Representatives. The crisis between the United States and Israel was defused.

But at that tense period of history, even the most seemingly innocent act involving Israel could result in an international incident. The planting of a tree in Israel had become a popular way to honor an individual on a special occasion. A contribution is made to the Jewish National Fund, which sends a certificate to the honoree announcing that a tree has been planted. The planting of such a tree by a Jewish friend to honor President Ford created a dilemma for the United States. This particular tree was planted south of Jerusalem on the West Bank, occupied by Israel after the 1967 war. The question of how to acknowledge the honor created a diplomatic crisis resulting in urgent consultation involving the State Department, the White House, and the National Security Council. General Brent Scowcroft, the president's national security adviser, wrote to the president: "Official U.S. endorsement of this activity would run contrary to our policy. We do not accept any changes in the Occupied Territories because their future is an issue of the negotiations. . . . It would not be appropriate for you to send a message to the dedication ceremonies of this tree which would appear to align you closely with Israeli policies on the future of the West Bank."[15]

The American ambassador in Israel even sent a confidential telegram to the secretary of state about the observations of embassy officials on the scene in Israel. After relating information about the establishment of Jewish settlements on occupied land, the ambassador reported that "tree planting, of course, is [the] traditional sign of permanency here."[16] The dilemma ended with President Ford writing a general letter of thanks to the donor without mentioning the location of the tree planting.

Today, the tree-planting affair seems almost silly. It was, however, indicative of the sensitivity of Middle East diplomacy and the difficulty of reaching a peaceful settlement. Speaking to a private gathering of Arab American leaders at the White House, Ford said, "I have spent much more time on the Middle East than any other single subject."[17] In June, President Ford met with Egyptian leader Anwar Sadat in Salzburg, Austria, and Israeli Prime Minister Rabin in Washington. He told both leaders that they "[could] not allow another failure." In a private meeting at the White House on June 16, Ford told Max Fisher he was "moderately encouraged" by the talks.[18] As a result, Henry Kissinger resumed his shuttle diplomacy in the Middle East.

Success came for Kissinger on September 1, 1975. After a grueling twelve-day shuttle between Jerusalem and Cairo, he supervised the signing of a historic interim agreement between Israel and Egypt, which became known as Sinai II. Both sides agreed that "the conflict between them . . . shall not be resolved by military force but by peaceful means." In addition to strict observance of the cease-fire, Israel agreed to withdraw from the oil fields it had occupied in the Sinai and to pull back from two strategic passes. In return, Israeli nonmilitary cargoes were to be permitted through the Suez Canal.

The agreement was a turning point in world history. "By reducing the dangers of military and economic warfare this agreement is of great significance for the well-being of every American," President Ford stated. He hoped it would "contribute to building the confidence between the two sides which is required if ultimate peace is to be achieved." Ford placed congratulatory telephone calls to

Henry Kissinger's "shuttle diplomacy" paid off on
September 1, 1975, when he supervised the signing
of a historic agreement between Israel and Egypt.
Here, Kissinger (left, with glasses) is greeted by
President Ford at Andrews Air Force Base upon
the return of the secretary of state.

Yitzhak Rabin and Anwar Sadat. In response, Rabin told Ford, "We appreciate very much the special relations that have been so significant in the past and the present between our two countries, and I am sure that what we have done there today will add a new dimension to the relations between our two countries."

The American Jewish community was delighted. Letters and telegrams of congratulations reached the White House from major Jewish organizations. On September 8, Max Fisher led a delegation of Jewish leaders to a White House meeting with the president. Ford told the group that the United States managed to avert a serious deterioration in the Arab-Israeli situation that could have resulted in yet another war.

At the heart of the agreement was a commitment by the United States to create the U.S. Sinai Support Mission. Two hundred American civilian technicians were to electronically monitor the peace at the Sinai's only two accessible passes, the Giddi and Mitla Passes. Their presence, Henry Kissinger said, "is a limited—but crucial—American responsibility. It was not a role we sought. We accepted it at the request of both sides only when it became totally clear that there would be no agreement without it and only on carefully limited terms. We agreed because failure would have posed grave risks for the United States." Congressional approval was necessary at a time when Americans were concerned about a deeper involvement in world affairs after the disastrous withdrawal from Vietnam. Writing to the speaker of the House, Carl Albert, President Ford stated that the agreement "will reduce the risks of war, create new opportunities for negotiating peace. . . . This Agreement is in the overall national interest of the United States." He impressed upon the speaker the need for fast congressional action. Approval came from both political parties.

Goodwill suffered a major setback on November 10, 1975. The General Assembly of the United Nations, by a vote of seventy-two to thirty-five with thirty-two abstentions, approved an Arab-sponsored resolution which equated "Zionism"—the movement of the Jewish people for a return to their ancient homeland—with "a form of racism." The resolution was supported by many developing and communist nations for political reasons. Not far from the surface was the fact that many of their national economies depended on the Arab oil-producing countries.

The immediate response from many corners of American society was strong and uncompromising. A Florida member of Congress said, "If this anti-Semitic resolution carries" he would seek a reassessment of American financial participation in the United Nations. United States delegate to the United Nations Daniel P. Moynihan spoke angrily to the General Assembly. "A great evil has been loosed upon the world. The abomination of anti-Semitism has been given the appearance of international sanction." President Ford issued a statement that said: "We deplore in the strongest terms the recent vote. . . . Such action undermines the principles upon which the United Nations is based." Adding their voices to the complaints of Jewish organizations, many other American groups stated their opposition to the UN resolution. The League of Women Voters stated that the resolution was "one of the worst mistakes the UN General Assembly has made to date." The national commander of the American Legion sent a telegram to the president urging "congressional action to make a reassessment of U.S. membership in the United Nations."

According to nationwide polls, American sympathy for Israel over the Arabs increased from 39 percent in November 1973 to 52 percent in January 1975. Of all U.S. foreign aid recipients, Israel was the most popular among Americans. Israel ranked among the top four nations, along with Canada, Mexico, and the Netherlands as a "friend" of the United States.

With a presidential election upcoming in 1976, Republicans focused on the 40 percent of American Jews (up from 17 percent in 1968) who had voted for Richard Nixon in the 1972 election. This was a significant shift. A confidential White House report stated: "Of all ethnic groups in this country, Jews take the most active interest in elections and vote more assiduously than almost any other population group. They also contribute heavily to campaigns and engage actively in work at both the national and state level. It is apparent that a policy which hurts or appears to hurt Israel and appeases Arab demands will carry a stiff political price in the United States, and a price which the Republican party should not be asked to pay."[19]

On June 27, 1976, the political posturing took a backseat to a real life-and-death drama. An Air France airliner en route from Tel Aviv to Paris was hijacked in Athens, Greece, and ordered to Entebbe, Uganda, by Palestinian terrorists. The world watched and wrung its hands in despair as Israelis and non-Israeli Jews were segregated at the airport by the terrorists. It reminded many of the treatment of Jews by the Nazis in World War II. Words of sympathy poured in to Israel, which had a strict policy of not giving in to terrorist demands. President Ford told Max Fisher, "We share Israel's anguish over the terrorist hijacking to Uganda and the situation of the Israeli and other hostages. We have done our best to try to save the lives of the hostages without suggesting that the terms of the terrorists be met."

While negotiations continued, a special Israeli military force planned a nearly impossible mission. In what was to become a model operation in the fight against terrorism, Israeli planes flew undetected into Entebbe Airport, overpowered the terrorists and Ugandan troops, and returned to Israel with all but one Jewish hostage. One Israeli soldier, Yonatan Netanyahu, was killed. Twenty years later his brother, Benjamin, became Israel's prime minister. The heroic action further enhanced Israel's reputation in the free world and underscored its policy of protecting its citizens to the fullest.

Just prior to the 1976 election, President Ford responded to a reporter's question on Middle East peace. "I say," Ford stated, "that any settlement in the Middle East should come from direct negotiations between Israel and the Arab nations." His Democratic opponent, Governor Jimmy Carter of Georgia, proposed the involvement of the Soviet Union and the United States.

Another reporter asked President Ford to reveal his thoughts about the possibility for a permanent peace in the Middle East. Ford answered, "It would be the most significant achievement and . . . that would be a hallmark for any President. I hope it is myself." It was not to be Ford's fate: Jimmy Carter was elected the next president of the United States, and it was he, not Ford, who would preside over the historic signing of a peace treaty between Israel and Egypt.

1982

. . . the American people believe it is right and it is in our American interest to be pro-Israel.

—Hyman Bookbinder

Until 1977, Menachem Begin and Anwar Sadat seemed the two most unlikely national leaders to share a Nobel Peace Prize. Sadat, who succeeded Gamal Abdel Nasser as president of Egypt, instigated the 1973 war with Israel. Begin succeeded Yitzhak Rabin to become the first non-Labor party leader of Israel. Since Israel's birth in 1948, the Labor party had been the only political party in power. It was the political home of each of Israel's leaders, from Ben-Gurion to Rabin.

For years Begin's hard-line, uncompromising positions on Jewish rights to Palestine had made him an outsider in Israeli politics. Similarly, his unyielding views on Arabs, the return of occupied territory, and the establishment of new Jewish settlements in the West Bank after the 1967 war caused jitters both in Israel and the United States. Prior to 1948, he was the leader of a Jewish underground group dedicated to driving the British out of Palestine at any cost.

For his violent zeal, the British targeted him as a terrorist and offered a reward for his capture. With the establishment of Israel in 1948, Begin settled in for a thirty-year role on the political sidelines as the scorned leader of the parliamentary opposition.

As young men, both Begin and Sadat had been jailed for their political views—Sadat in Egypt, Begin in Russia. Sadat had a rural childhood in Egypt, as Begin had in Russia. Sadat was an observant Muslim and Begin a religious Jew. They both moved to larger cities to further their education—Sadat to Cairo, Begin to Warsaw, Poland. Sadat became a military officer, and Begin joined the Polish army. Throughout their careers each man suffered vicious personal attacks from their critics. In spite of similar experiences as outsiders, each had sharply differing views on the Middle East muddle. Their differences would soon be reconciled by a third outsider, Jimmy Carter, the largely unknown, deeply religious former governor of Georgia who succeeded Gerald Ford as president of the United States in the 1976 election.

Criticism of the Labor government's handling of the 1973 Yom Kippur War and charges of corruption had created political turmoil in Israel. Yet, it was to the surprise of nearly everyone that Menachem Begin and his right-wing opposition coalition, the Likud, swept to victory in the 1977 election. During the intense election campaigning, the Likud called for the right of Jews to settle anywhere in the occupied West Bank and Gaza. They opposed the "Land for Peace" policies of the previous Labor governments. Interestingly, some analysts credited the Menachem Begin victory to the perceived pro-Palestinian views of President Jimmy Carter.

Two months before the Israeli election, President Jimmy Carter, speaking at a town-meeting forum in Clinton, Massachusetts, endorsed the idea of a "homeland" for the Palestinian people. Prime Minister Begin echoed the feeling of most Israelis that a Palestinian state would be "a dagger struck at the heart of Israel." They felt that sharing a common border with a Palestinian state would only result in increased terrorism. Reaction from the American Jewish community was so negative that the president had to quickly soften his original statement. His revision called for a Palestinian "entity" to be aligned with Jordan and not be an "independent" state.

Since assuming office in January 1977, Carter had placed the Middle East at the top of his foreign policy list. Early in his presidency, Carter dispatched his new secretary of state, Cyrus Vance, to the Middle East. In March 1977, Prime Minister Yitzhak Rabin visited Washington. While Rabin preferred a comprehensive peace treaty, Carter supported direct talks with the PLO and a substantial return of land by Israel in exchange for peace. Before discussions could continue, the 1977 Israeli election boosted Menachem Begin and the Likud party to power.

In the months that followed, Sadat and Begin separately visited Washington to explore possibilities of peace. In April, Sadat told Carter that relations with Israel could be "normalized." He repeated his belief again in July in a speech before the U.S. Congress. Speaking to his own parliament in Cairo on July 16, 1977, Sadat announced that he was prepared to recognize Israel once a formal peace treaty was signed. Secretary Vance returned to the Middle East to keep the peace momentum alive by encouraging both Egypt and Israel to make concessions.

In an effort to energize the discussions, President Carter and the Soviet Union issued a joint statement calling for a conference in Geneva, Switzerland, to discuss a comprehensive settlement of the Arab-Israeli problem. The conference, which would include Palestinian representation, would explore Israeli withdrawal from Arab territories occupied in the 1967 war and the "legitimate rights of the Palestinian people."

The proposal met with opposition from both Egypt and Israel. Egypt, which had earlier expelled Soviet military advisers for interfering in Egypt's government affairs, did not trust the Soviets. Israel, angry that the United States, under provisions of the Sinai Accords, did not consult the Jewish state in advance, dismissed the idea as "unacceptable." Begin's Labor party opponents called the American-Soviet statement "unprecedented, unnecessary, ill-timed, and ill-phrased." The call for a Geneva conference only hardened Israel's attitude against negotiations. Even as Israel and Egypt continued discussions with the United States on convening a Geneva meeting, they sought a way to politely decline the opportunity. The White House was quickly bombarded with thousands of telegrams and letters from American Jewish leaders and members of Congress who also distrusted the plan.

In an attempt to keep the idea of a Geneva conference alive, President Carter sent a personal handwritten appeal to President Sadat on October 21, 1977. "I need your help," Carter wrote. "The time has now come to move forward, and your early public endorsement of our approach is extremely important—perhaps vital—in advancing all parties to Geneva. This is a personal appeal for your support." Carter and Sadat had begun a friendly relationship shortly after Carter's inauguration. "Peace in the Middle East was a major concern for me," Carter later wrote. After the mid-1977 Israeli elections, Prime Minister Begin was also welcomed at the White House. Begin and Sadat both trusted President Carter. Sadat remarked that he trusted the American president because Carter was "a farmer like me."

Carter, Sadat, and Begin had little in common other than firmly rooted religious beliefs and the realization that the only solution for the Middle East cycle of violence was a meaningful peace, despite the fact that both Sadat and Begin had been supporters of violence in their earlier years. Neither was happy with President Carter's involvement of the Soviet Union for a Middle East summit meeting in Geneva. But neither wanted to offend their well-meaning friend, Jimmy Carter. It was Anwar Sadat who took matters in his own hands and came up with a stunning plan. Addressing his parliament in Cairo on November 9, 1977, Sadat matter-of-factly announced, "I am ready to go to their house, to the Knesset, to discuss peace with the Israeli leaders." No one expected what came next. Recognizing the historic opportunity, Menachem Begin immediately sent Sadat a personal invitation to visit Jerusalem.

At 8:00 P.M. on November 19, 1977, an Egyptian airliner landed at Israel's Ben-Gurion Airport. As television cameras broadcast the moment to the world, Anwar Sadat was graciously welcomed by Prime Minister Begin and a committee of distinguished Israelis. The visit produced unforgettable images, including Begin and Sadat clasping hands and pledging "No more war!"; Sadat warmly greeting his former enemy, Golda Meir; and Sadat addressing the Knesset. ". . . In sincerity," he told the legislators and the millions watching worldwide, "I tell you that we welcome you among us with all security and safety." The Israelis were giddy with joy. For the first time since independence in 1948, the leader of an Arab country (still technically at war with Israel) had visited the Jewish state with an offer of peace. Although Sadat and Begin were not even close to any meaningful agreements, they had broken the barrier of hate that had separated their peoples for thirty years and begun a dialogue on peace. Both leaders agreed that a Geneva conference might be an ideal place to sign a peace treaty, but the negotiations leading to that treaty had to be concluded by Egypt and Israel alone.

Anwar Sadat returned home to Egypt a hero to many of his own people. To the other Arab nations, however, he was a traitor. A month after Sadat's triumphant visit to Jerusalem, Menachem Begin was formally received by Sadat in Ismaillya, Egypt. In the months that followed, both sides continued to debate the possibilities of a negotiated peace. There were no easy solutions. The Egyptians wanted the return of all occupied lands, while the Israelis were deeply concerned about their own security. Begin's supporters in Israel and the United States were opposed to any "land for peace" deal with the Egyptians.

This hard-line attitude created friction with the United States and segments of the American Jewish community. Of greatest concern was the policy of the Begin government supporting new Jewish settlements in the West Bank and Gaza. Meanwhile, Palestinian guerrilla attacks continued to inflame Israel. In a particularly bloody incident, 34 Israelis were killed and 74 wounded by guerrillas who came ashore south of Haifa. In retaliation, Israeli forces crossed the Lebanese border with 20,000 troops to root out Palestinian terrorists.

The travel lanes between Washington and the Middle East flowed in both directions. Sadat and Begin visited Washington frequently as Secretary of State Vance, taking a page from Henry Kissinger's diplomatic handbook, regularly flew to Cairo and Jerusalem. Although Israel welcomed the assistance of the United States, Israelis felt the Carter administration leaned too far in support of Egyptian views. The discussions, often tough and uncompromising, did not lead to any agreements. Something dramatic would be needed to move the parties to meaningful agreements.

In August 1978, President Carter sent Secretary Vance on yet another trip to Cairo and Jerusalem. This time, Vance carried with him separate handwritten letters from President Carter for Begin and Sadat. "It is imperative," Carter wrote Begin, "that every effort be made to capitalize on this unprecedented opportunity to consummate a definitive peace treaty between Israel and Egypt. . . ." The president invited both leaders to join him at Camp David, the presidential retreat in the Maryland hills, for a series of private talks with "maximum direct contact" between Sadat and Begin. "I look forward," Carter said, "to an early opportunity to consider with you again one of the most important and challenging issues ever decided by political leaders." On August 8 the White House issued a statement announcing the conference, "not because the chances for peace are now so high, but because the stakes in peace are very high and because the risks, in fact, have risen."[1]

The conference began on September 5. Surrounded by aides, cooks, secretaries, and the lush autumn foliage, the participants settled in for what they imagined would be a three- or four-day marathon. Twelve days later, the bedraggled leaders finally reached a historic agreement on an Egyptian-Israeli peace treaty. The negotiating process had been tiring and at times confrontational. It could not have succeeded without Jimmy Carter, who shuttled between Sadat's and Begin's Camp David lodges seeking compromises and understanding.

The talks did not begin well. Menachem Begin was rigid and unyielding in his security concerns. Anwar Sadat was insistent that no agreement was possible without a total Israeli withdrawal from all occupied territory. There was a definite need for compromise. Carter quickly understood that Begin and Sadat were "personally incompatible." The president realized that "it would be better if each of them spoke to me as the mediator instead of directly to the other."[2] For the last ten days of the negotiations both Middle East leaders were kept apart while President Carter went from one to the other. The discussions deteriorated to the point that Sadat would have left were it not for the intense pressure to stay applied by Carter. Begin had been considered the most unlikely Israeli leader to give up occupied land. Yet, in the end, Begin realized that the conference would fail if Israel refused to withdraw from the Sinai or not recognize the "legitimate rights of the Palestinians." While Israel agreed to remove from the Sinai all Jewish settlements and turn over oil fields and military airfields,

*Jimmy Carter (left) and Menachem Begin share a
light moment during the Camp David Peace Accords.
Although Carter was able to get along with both Begin
and Anwar Sadat, the president quickly determined
that the leaders of Israel and Egypt themselves were
"personally incompatible."*

the Egyptians agreed to sign a separate peace treaty with Israel without regard for the views of other Arab states or the Palestinians.

The three leaders flew by helicopter to the White House on September 17. "There are still great difficulties," Carter said, "that remain and many hard issues to be settled." Sadat, speaking of President Carter, said, "He worked harder than our forefathers did in Egypt building the pyramids!" At the signing ceremony for the Camp David Accords, Sadat and Begin initialed two documents with Jimmy Carter affixing his signature as witness. The Camp David Accords broke the cycle of distrust between Egypt and Israel and set an example for other Arab states to follow.

The first document, the "Framework for Peace in the Middle East," affirmed the beginning of additional negotiations to settle the future of the West Bank and the Gaza Strip. The second document, the "Framework for the Conclusion of a Peace Treaty Between Egypt and Israel," laid out a timetable for the opening of diplomatic relations between the two countries within three months and phased Israeli withdrawal from the Sinai within three years. The documents called for all parties to seek peace founded on "respect for sovereignty, territorial integrity, and political independence of every state in the area and their right to live in peace within secure and recognized boundaries free from threats or acts of force."

The details of the peace were hammered out by diplomats from both sides with the help of the United States. Key stumbling blocks for the Israelis were the future of Israel's energy supply and the cost of replacing the military bases in the Sinai scheduled to be handed over to Egypt.

Months of fruitless negotiations and frequent disagreements, however, had led to a downward spiral in United States–Israel relations. To break the impasse and ensure passage of the treaty by Israel's parliament, Jimmy Carter traveled to Cairo and Jerusalem in early March 1979. With Carter's prodding, Israel and Egypt agreed to a date by which both countries would exchange ambassadors. The United States also guaranteed oil supplies to Israel for fifteen years, together with additional military and economic aid including the building of two air bases in the Negev to replace those abandoned to Egypt in the Sinai.

On March 26, 1979, Sadat and Begin, with Carter as witness, signed a peace treaty on the White House lawn—the first treaty ever between Israel and an Arab country. As

Carter later addressed a joint session of Congress to provide details, Begin and Sadat observed proudly from the Visitor's Gallery of the House of Representatives. Speaking of Carter, Sadat said, "Without any exaggeration what he did constitutes one of the greatest achievements of our time." Carter, in turn, was more subdued. "We have won, at last, the first step of peace, a first step on a long and difficult road." Omitted from the treaty was any decision related to the future of the West Bank, Gaza, the Golan Heights, or East Jerusalem. The Israelis did, however, agree to give limited autonomy to the Palestinians in Gaza and the West Bank. In spite of continuing violent reactions by Palestinians in the occupied territories, both Israel and Egypt continued to honor their treaty agreements. For Americans, the treaty offered proof that the country's national strength went beyond strong military proficiency. "This peace treaty," a presidential aide wrote, "was the product not only of Israeli and Egyptian wisdom but of American power."

While most of the world at large greeted the treaty with great satisfaction, most of the Arab world was appalled that Egypt had signed a treaty with "the Zionist enemy." The Arab League moved its headquarters from Egypt to Tunisia and urged its member states to withdraw their ambassadors from Cairo. Palestinian voices in Gaza and the West Bank also decried the treaty.

Despite the negative opinions, the peace treaty held. It reduced the dangers of general war in the area and turned the Middle East toward peace. A few months after the signing of the Camp David Accords, Sadat and Begin were honored with the Nobel Peace Prize. Even when actions by Israel inflamed the Arab world, such as the 1980 annexation of East Jerusalem as a permanent part of the city, Egypt kept its word.

On October 6, 1981, Anwar Sadat was assassinated by Islamic fundamentalists in Egypt during a military parade.

While President Carter was lauded for his part in the talks that resulted in a historic peace treaty between Israel and Egypt, he was humble about his accomplishments, calling the treaty "a first step on a long and difficult road." Here, Carter (center), Sadat (left), and Begin (right) stand together during the treaty-signing ceremony on March 26, 1979.

They were upset with Sadat's pro-Western attitudes and the liberalization of the Egyptian economy, which resulted in increased poverty for many. The rise of Muslim extremist groups led to increased criticism of the government and calls for the assassination of Sadat. Although the fundamentalists opposed the peace treaty with Israel, support for the agreement was continued by Sadat's successor, Hosni Mubarak.

In the presidential election of 1980, Jimmy Carter had been defeated by Ronald Reagan. Carter's success in bringing Israel and Egypt together was temporarily forgotten as Americans coped with a worsening economic situation and the embarrassment of having American diplomats held captive by an Islamic fundamentalist government in Iran. In spite of Carter's success in bringing about the peace treaty, many American Jews still questioned his commitment to Israel and the wisdom of Israel returning land to Egypt. Furthermore, when the Carter administration proposed to sell state-of-the-art jet fighter planes to Saudi Arabia and Egypt, American Jewish leaders united in political action against the president. When Carter's White House liaison with the Jewish community, Mark Siegel, appeared at a meeting of Jewish leaders to explain the administration's view, he was roundly booed and hissed. In response, he resigned from his position. Even when changes were made to include Israel in the proposal, fierce lobbying against the sale engulfed Congress. "This is going to be a very tough legislative fight," a presidential adviser said. The president ultimately won the fight but lost the political and financial support of American Jews for his reelection campaign. Carter received only 45 percent of the Jewish vote in the 1980 election, an all-time low for a Democratic candidate.

President Ronald Reagan inherited the results of Jimmy Carter's negotiated peace. The newly elected president was a longtime friend of Israel. As a candidate for the presidency, he had said, "The Holy Land is the Holy Land to a great many of us. All of us in America go back in our ancestry to some other part of the world. There is no nation like us, except Israel."

Reagan proposed a special "Memorandum of Understanding," which, he said, would "reaffirm the common bonds of friendship between the United States and Israel." The economic and military benefits of this formal agreement would reassure Israel of the continued support of the

United States. But that bond was soon to weaken. From inside the administration, opposition came mainly from Secretary of Defense Caspar Weinberger. "In military policy the United States is not going to be hostage to Israel," Weinberger stated. The secretary's goal was to sell Arab countries more advanced missiles and airplanes to reassure them of America's "balanced view" of the Middle East. The most controversial part of the 1981 plan was to sell $8 million worth of AWACS (airborne warning and control system aircraft) to Saudi Arabia. These new planes were flying radar stations able to spot incoming airplanes and missiles 350 miles (564 kilometers) away.

For Israel and its American supporters, the AWACS sale posed a real danger to the Jewish state. Working through AIPAC, an intense lobbying effort by supporters of Israel focused on both houses of Congress. In spite of his previous support of Israel, the president fought back. He was caught up in the wider implications of the deal. Later, recalling the situation, Reagan wrote, "I believed that it was a battle that had to be won. If we lost on AWACS we might undermine our ability to persuade Congress to approve our domestic programs and the rearmament of the Pentagon."[3] Newspapers simply described the lobbying effort as a choice between Reagan or Begin. After weeks of intense lobbying, the AWACS bill passed the Senate by just four votes. Reagan had won, and the much feared Israeli lobby had lost.

Events in the Middle East also contributed to the breakdown of the Memorandum of Understanding. Early in 1981, Israeli intelligence confirmed that Iraq's French-built nuclear reactor at Osirak, 10 miles (16 kilometers) from Baghdad, Saudi Arabia, would soon be operational. In spite of Iraq's claim that the reactor was to be used for peaceful purposes, Israel knew that it was capable of producing the necessary material to make nuclear bombs. As early as 1975, Iraqi leader Saddam Hussein was quoted as saying that his nuclear program was "the first Arab attempt toward nuclear arming."[4] Another Iraqi leader said two years later, "The Arabs must get a bomb." Israel could not allow one of its archenemies to have that power.

On June 7, 1981, sixteen Israeli warplanes swept low over the desert of Saudi Arabia to avoid Arab radar, entered Iraqi airspace, and bombed the nuclear reactor at Osirak. The daring, well-coordinated attack surprised the world. Although many countries were relieved that the Iraqi nuclear threat was at least temporarily stopped, international condemnation of Israel followed. The United States was angry that American-built planes had been used. Other countries were upset that Israel had flown over the airspace of neighboring countries without permission. Menachem Begin brushed aside these complaints. "Israel has nothing to apologize for," he said, "ours is a just cause, we stand by it, and it will triumph."

On December 14, 1981, in another act that angered the United States and the world community, Begin annexed the Golan Heights, the scene of fierce fighting in preceding wars with Syria. Israel had captured the geographically important area from Syria in 1967 and enlarged its rule of the Golan during the 1973 war. When the Golan had been under Syrian control, the mountainous region was a launching area for artillery and missile attacks on northern Israeli settlements. President Reagan, angry at not being consulted in advance by Begin, canceled the Memorandum of Understanding. An equally angry Begin called in the American ambassador, Samuel Lewis, and complained bitterly that the United States was not treating Israel fairly as an independent nation. "Are we a vassal state? Are we a banana republic?"

In early June 1982, Israel's ambassador to Great Britain was shot on a London street by a Palestinian terrorist. This was the final straw for Israel. In retaliation for that attempted assassination, the increased number of Palestinian terrorist raids into Israel, and indiscriminate shelling of

Israeli settlements in the north, Israel invaded Lebanon on June 6. Lebanon had become a center of revolutionary activity. It was further torn apart by civil unrest as radical Palestinian paramilitary groups set up bases in the country from which to attack Israel. Soon, the elected government of Lebanon was overwhelmed and fell apart. Anarchy ruled. With the Lebanese government unable to control events, Israel decided to intervene to protect its own citizens.

Israel called the invasion "Operation Peace for Galilee." In the preceding years, the Lebanese government had virtually ceased to control the movements of Palestinian guerrillas on its soil. The country was torn by civil insurrection at all levels. The army's mission was to seek out and destroy PLO guerrillas based in Lebanon. In a coordinated military move, which again earned Israel worldwide condemnation, Israel attacked with massive firepower from the air and on the ground.

Advancing into the outskirts of Beirut, Israel pounded the Lebanese capital to dislodge the heavily entrenched PLO guerrillas hidden among innocent civilians. Day after day, American television broadcast the bloody images of war, including shots of women and children forced from their burning homes. President Reagan urged an end to the fighting, but the Israelis continued to advance. A two-month siege of Beirut resulted in heavy casualties for the Israelis. In Israel, opposition to the military operation increased as well-respected Israelis condemned Begin's invasion of Lebanon. Abba Eban, former ambassador to the United States, said, "This war is already on the way to becoming the most traumatic of all the Israeli experiences." He didn't realize how true his prophecy would be.

As the bombing of Beirut increased, President Reagan became furious. Picking up the telephone, he called the Israeli prime minister. "Menachem," Reagan told Begin, "this is a holocaust." Begin angrily responded, "Mr. President, I think I know what a Holocaust is!" But after reflecting on the American president's plea, Begin ordered an end to the bombing.

President Reagan encouraged other countries to join with the United States and form a multinational force (MNF) to enter Lebanon and provide a buffer between Israelis and Palestinians. It would also allow a peaceful withdrawal of PLO guerrillas. On August 25, eight hundred U.S. Marines joined three hundred French paratroopers in West Beirut.

Israel's bombings destroyed the PLO's Beirut headquarters and eventually forced the Palestinian guerrillas from Lebanon. The U.S. Marines were withdrawn on September 10 in spite of the ongoing conflict among Lebanese political factions. While Israel may have succeeded at great human cost to dislodge the PLO, it failed to convince the world of the importance of this mission and suffered a public-relations disaster in the United States. The low point for Israel occurred between September 16 and 18, 1982. Members of a Lebanese militia allied with Israel, angered at the killing of the newly elected Lebanese president, entered two Palestinian refugee camps, Sabra and Shatila. What ensued was a systematic, indiscriminate killing of men, women, and children.

Television cameras broadcast the bloody aftermath to homes worldwide. President Reagan issued a statement of "outrage and revulsion over the murders." Although the killings were carried out by Lebanese, the finger of blame pointed at Israel, which was in overall control of the camps and should have carefully monitored the actions of its Lebanese allies. Prior to Israel's march into Lebanon, American public opinion was sympathetic to Israel's cause. After Sabra and Shatila, 70 percent of Americans agreed that Begin's policies were hurting support for Israel in the United States. On September 15, 1983, Menachem Begin resigned as Israel's prime minister after serving more than six years.

He was succeeded by another Likud member, Yitzhak Shamir, who, like Begin, was a political hard-liner.

Ronald Reagan later recalled his relations with the former Israeli leader. "My heart went out especially to Begin," he recalled. "I had many difficulties with him while I was President, but he was an Israeli patriot devoted above all to the survival of his country."[5] In spite of the bad news from Lebanon, President Reagan tried to breathe life into a peace plan for the Middle East. The Reagan Plan, unveiled in September, called for "self government by the Palestinians of the West Bank and Gaza in association with Jordan." Despite private assurances to Begin that the United States would not require the removal of Israeli settlements from the West Bank, Israel rejected the plan. So did the Palestinians. That month also, an Arab summit held in Fez, Morocco, came up with its own plan, which called for the withdrawal of Israel from all territory captured during the 1967 war, including East Jerusalem, the removal of all Israeli settlements from the West Bank, and the establishment of a Palestinian state.

On Yitzhak Shamir's first official visit to Washington on November 29, 1983, President Reagan offered Israel a special "free trade" agreement. "I am pleased to announce," said Reagan, "that we have agreed to establish a Joint Political-Military Group to examine ways in which we can enhance Israeli-American cooperation." The agreement built on existing intelligence programs, which brought together the American FBI and CIA with Israel's intelligence agency, the Mossad. The United States supplied Israel with the latest in weaponry, while Israel shared Soviet weapons captured in battle from its Arab neighbors. Unfortunately, this upturn in relations took an embarrassing turn for Israel two years later.

The November 1985 arrest of Jonathan Jay Pollard and his wife, Anne Henderson Pollard, by the FBI outside the gate of the Israeli Embassy in Washington shook the very foundation of the relationship between the United States and Israel. Pollard, a civilian security analyst for U.S. Naval Intelligence, was accused of passing top-secret American intelligence documents to Israel. Beginning in 1984, Pollard began providing classified documents to Israeli agents. By the time of his arrest, the FBI calculated that Pollard had turned over a literal mountain of valuable intelligence information, including satellite photos of military installations. The documents included information that permitted Israel to avoid enemy radar and launch a daring air raid, which destroyed PLO headquarters in Tunisia.

Pollard, who from his youth was an ardent supporter of Israel, became a spy when he feared that the United States was not supplying its ally, Israel, with enough meaningful intelligence to maintain military superiority in the Middle East. His idealistic concern for Israel's survival was shared by many in the United States. But most supporters of Israel were aghast that an American would go so far as to commit espionage. Yitzhak Rabin called Pollard's action "a real disaster, a real wound in Israeli-U.S. relations."

Spying on other countries is not a rare occurrence. Yet this case was unique for several reasons, including the huge amount of documents that were transferred and the fact that Israel was a close ally of the United States and each country had agreed not to spy on the other. Secretary of Defense Caspar Weinberger said, "It is difficult for me to conceive of a greater harm to national security than that caused by the defendant in view of the breadth, the critical importance of the United States, and the high sensitivity of the information he sold to Israel." Anne Henderson said, "I feel my husband and I did what we were expected to do, what our moral obligation was as Jews and human beings, and I have no regrets about that."

Jonathan Pollard was sentenced to life imprisonment. Many think the punishment did not fit the crime and continue to fight for a reconsideration of the tough sentence. In a television interview in 1988, Jonathan Pollard tried to justify his actions. "I had become aware of Mr. Weinberger's agenda in Washington in regard to Israel. . . . It was fundamentally to place Israel in a position where she would be forced to make an unenviable choice between a ruinous war or shameful peace." Yitzhak Shamir called the Pollard affair a "human tragedy" that should not be allowed to affect the ongoing relationship with the United States. "We are intent," he said, "on maintaining and developing our close and friendly ties . . . and the United States has informed us that they share this feeling completely."

The regular cycle of Middle East violence continued and extended to other sites. PLO terrorists killed Israeli visitors in Cyprus, shot up European airports, commandeered airliners, and on October 7, 1985, hijacked a Mediterranean cruise ship, the *Achille Lauro*. In an act that resulted in worldwide revulsion, the terrorists killed and threw the body of an elderly, wheelchair-bound American, Leon Klinghoffer, into the sea. The PLO seemed to be under the control of violent extremists. In that atmosphere, Yasir Arafat found it difficult to focus his Palestine Liberation Organization on a peaceful solution. Then came the Intifada.

A NEW ERA

Enough of blood and tears.

—Yitzhak Rabin

Israel, with a population of about 5.4 million, is approximately the size of New Jersey. In contrast to its size, Israel receives more national newspaper space and broadcast news time than most American states. This attention is partly due to American public interest in the region and partly due to the number of foreign journalists who frequently travel to or are based in Israel. There is always something happening in the small country.

As the only true democracy in the Middle East, Israel shares many similarities with the United States. English is widely spoken and understood. Rush-hour traffic jams create daily gridlock in Tel Aviv, and supermarket shoppers pass shelves filled with familiar American brands. Israel is a comfortable place for foreign reporters to live while they cover the Middle East. Like America, Israel has an open society with a lively press whose newspapers represent every possible opinion.

When it is midmorning in New York, it is already late afternoon in Jerusalem. Sunday in Israel is a normal workday. Schools, businesses, and government offices are all open. Muslims observe their day of rest on Friday, while Saturday is the Jewish Sabbath. In the United States, weekends are normally quiet news periods. But thanks to modern satellite communications, Americans can tune in to any of the Sunday morning network news programs and probably see a live report from Israel. "We are hosts to the largest press corps in the world after Washington," said Chaim Herzog, the president of Israel.

Over the years, American viewers have grown familiar with all aspects of Israeli life. Reports on the numerous wars, terrorist raids, and diplomatic shuttling were augmented by human-interest stories on everyday life. By and large, the visual images of a Western-style country under siege consciously and unconsciously affected the way Americans thought of Israel. Reports from Arab countries were much less frequent and less diverse since many Arab leaders, not comfortable with a free press, Western customs, and English fluency, had difficulty in getting their message across.

But the way Americans thought of Israel changed dramatically in December 1987 with the beginning of a popular Palestinian uprising—the Intifada—against Israeli occupation in the West Bank and Gaza. The disillusionment of young Palestinians with their own leadership and with Israel led to the sudden eruption of pent-up rage. Armed mainly with stones, young people attacked Israeli soldiers, who responded to the spontaneous rebellion with bullets, arrests, and curfews. As the Intifada escalated and became a way of life, the number of Palestinian casualties rose.

In its attempt to quell the violence, Israel lost its "underdog" standing in world opinion. Journalists seemed to appear at every confrontation between Israeli soldiers and Palestinians. Newspaper photographs and video clips showing Israeli soldiers reacting to Palestinian provocations negatively affected American perceptions of Israel. President Herzog said that the foreign reporters were "not showing the whole picture" and were presenting their stories with "complete imbalance." Herzog also complained that the journalists themselves, with their cameras and sound equipment, helped incite some of the violence as the leaders of the uprising relished the media attention. As an American rabbi put it, "The problem of TV coverage is that the TV camera does not record history, it makes history." Many American Jewish leaders felt that news reports from Israel usually suffered from a lack of historical understanding and focused on the single dramatic event of the moment. Little they said could diminish the power of the pictures.

Israel found itself fighting a battle on two fronts: the streets of the West Bank and the world's news media. An Israeli Foreign Ministry official said, "A child throwing a stone at a soldier who is armed gets sympathy, even though he is committing a violent act." Israel's defense minister, Yitzhak Rabin, complained, "When the Iraqis killed five thousand Kurds with gas bombs, I did not see anything in the world media comparable to the reaction of Israel's using sticks against Palestinians. The world's response was totally out of proportion to Israel's actions."

Sensing the Intifada as a remarkable opportunity to shape events, the PLO assumed control of the disorganized stone throwers and turned the Intifada into a full-scale political campaign to achieve a Palestinian state in the West Bank and Gaza. The action spurred diplomatic movement. King Hussein of Jordan, who had seized the West Bank of Palestine during the 1948 war and lost it to the Israelis in 1967, renounced his claims to the occupied land. "The independent Palestinian state," he said, "will be established on the occupied Palestinian land after its liberation."

The Palestinians took full advantage of their new situation. Although some factions of the Palestine Liberation Organization such as Hamas supported increased terrorism against Israel, most groups within the PLO agreed with Yasir Arafat that the time had come to pursue peace. It would not be easy. Few Israelis trusted the Palestinians, and the United States, siding with Israel, continued a long-standing policy of not speaking with PLO representatives. On November 15, 1988, the leaders of the PLO convened in Algeria and declared the establishment of a Palestinian state. They also voted to recognize Israel, renounce terrorism, and accept UN Resolution 242, the territory for peace initiative. The United States quickly opened lines of communication with the PLO but just as quickly broke them off a few months later when Palestinian terrorists launched an unsuccessful raid on Israel. Israeli voters were also not convinced of the PLO's sincerity and, in 1988, reelected Yitzhak Shamir and his hard-line Likud party.

The election of President George Bush in 1988 marked another turning point for the Middle East. Like their predecessors, Bush and his secretary of state, James Baker, set out to bring peace to the Middle East. But unlike the pro-Israel Reagan presidency, the Bush administration displayed other sympathies. Speaking in 1989 to AIPAC, Secretary Baker repeated his solution to the Middle East problem. He called on Israel's Arab neighbors to "stop the challenges to Israel's standing in international organizations" and then admonished Israel to "stop settlement activity [and] reach out to the Palestinians as neighbors who deserve political rights." To Israel, Baker's words were meaningless since they required Israel to make substantial concessions without any guarantee of ultimate peace.

Although Israel agreed with the United States on the need for peace in the Middle East, Yitzhak Shamir and the American Jewish community largely opposed the ideas of the Bush administration. Before it signed any agreements and relinquished any more territory, Israel wanted iron-clad assurances of a meaningful peace and normal relations with its neighbors.

Relations between Israel and the United States reached an all-time low. At the UN, the United States, often Israel's sole defender on the Security Council, joined other members to condemn Israel for incidents against Palestinians. Harsh talk from the secretary of state convinced Shamir that the Bush administration was committed to a Middle East policy that did not automatically support Israel.

Shamir ignored Bush's efforts at peace. As the Intifada violence against Israelis continued to rage, Israeli reaction toughened. Israelis were in no mood for dialogue while their citizens were under attack. An Israeli spokesman said, "We've shown that we don't knuckle under to pressure." In spite of the difficulties, support for Israel in Congress remained strong. In 1990 the Senate voted overwhelmingly for a $3 billion aid package.

Ironically, it was a real war that led to peace. On August 2, 1990, Iraq invaded the neighboring country of Kuwait. The world was shocked and surprised. The United Nations reacted with a series of punishing resolutions, which targeted Iraq's aggression. Trade embargoes, including the use of force to stop shipping to Iraq and a curtailment of Iraq's important oil exports, put a stranglehold on the country's economy. Iraq's leader, Saddam Hussein, ignored the pressure, including the United Nations resolution authorizing member countries to "use all necessary means" to force Iraq to withdraw from Kuwait.

The United States took a leadership role in the worldwide effort against Iraq. Reasons for American concern were complex. First, Iraq's brazen aggression against a peaceful neighbor could not be permitted to succeed. Second, the Persian Gulf was a major source of oil upon which Western countries were dependent. Any disruption of the flow would greatly affect world economic conditions.

While diplomatic discussions with Iraq dragged on without success, the United States, at the invitation of Saudi

Arabia, prepared for a military solution to the problem. As a force assembled in Saudi Arabia to carry out "Operation Desert Storm," Secretary of State Baker met in Geneva, Switzerland, with Iraq's foreign minister in an attempt to prevent hostilities. The Iraqis were not convinced that the United States would actually fight.

On January 16, 1991, the United States began the first of a series of massive air raids on Iraq's capital, Baghdad, and military targets throughout the country. The following day Iraq launched the first wave of SCUD missile attacks against Israel, a country not involved in the international coalition against Iraq. A total of eight missiles were fired; three landed in Israel's largest city, Tel Aviv.

Iraq was a long-standing enemy of Israel. It remained the only 1948 attacker of Israel not to have signed an armistice agreement and was still legally at war with "the Zionist entity." Israel, although pleased to see its enemy in trouble, had been convinced by President Bush not to join the worldwide military coalition against Iraq, which included a number of Arab nations. Iraq's firing of SCUD missiles against Israel was a calculated effort to force Israeli retaliation. Iraq knew that Israel had never before held back military retaliation for any attack. Yet, if Israel responded, the fragile coalition against Iraq would have fallen apart. Hatred of Israel was so great that no Arab nation could risk cooperating with Israel to attack Iraq.

On a near daily basis during the Gulf War, Americans sat glued to their television screens and watched as Israeli families, wearing grotesque gas masks, huddled in sealed rooms. The precautions the Israelis took were deadly serious, as Iraq had threatened Israel with poison gas attacks. (Since Israel's 1981 destruction of Iraq's nuclear reactor at Osirak, Iraq had built up a stockpile of poison gas.) The thirty-nine SCUD missiles that hit Israel during the war were targeted at its major civilian centers, but casualties

Convinced by President George Bush to stay out of the coalition against Iraq and thus out of the Gulf War, Israel nevertheless became a target of Iraq, whose tactic was to goad Israel into retaliation. If Israel did retaliate, Iraqi leaders knew that the coalition against their country would fall apart, as it contained many Middle Eastern countries that were considered enemies of Israel. In this picture, an American Patriot missile is fired to intercept an Iraqi SCUD missile over Tel Aviv.

were relatively light and, fortunately, none of the bombs bore poison gas or chemicals.

Israel's destruction of Iraq's nuclear reactor, widely condemned at the time of the Osirak attack, turned out to be a strategic advantage to the allied coalition in 1991. Vice President Dan Quayle later said that if it were not for Israel, "Saddam Hussein might well have had the nuclear bomb by the time he invaded Kuwait and attacked Israel." Denied the means of producing nuclear weapons, the Iraqis had to rely on more-conventional arms. President Bush telephoned Prime Minister Shamir frequently during the war to assure him of U.S. support and, at the same time, to ensure that Israel's anger did not result in an independent attack on Iraq. Israel was anxious to join the battle but restricted itself to behind-the-scenes aid to the allies. Israel provided the United States with unmanned airborne vehicles to gather intelligence, mine plows to clear paths for allied troops, improvements to American aircraft, special night-vision goggles, and use of the port of Haifa.

The United States quickly dispatched Patriot missile batteries, operated by American soldiers, to Israel. The missiles were designed to intercept and destroy incoming offensive missiles. Israel was anxious to defend its own citizens by retaliating against Iraq. President Bush understood Israel's desire to hit back at Iraq but strongly cautioned Israel to refrain from any involvement in the war. He hoped that the Patriot missiles would provide Israel with needed feelings of security. On February 23 the massive ground war began. The coalition troops, led by the United States, effectively took the offensive, and by February 27 the war was over.

The United States tried to take advantage of the cooperative spirit of the coalition to pursue a meaningful peace between Israel and its neighbors. Speaking on television to the American people, President Bush said, "Ahead of us is the difficult task of securing a potentially historic peace [in the Middle East]." To reassure Israel, which had temporarily reassumed its image as a beleaguered country, American Secretary of Defense Richard Cheney visited in May 1991. At a press conference with his Israeli counterpart, Cheney said, "I reaffirmed to Moshe Arens the absolutely unshakable U.S. commitment to Israeli security, and also emphasized the enormous importance that the United States places upon the strategic relationship with Israel. We think that relationship is as strong and as important today as it has ever been and that the cooperation that we were able to engage in during the war in the Gulf and in dealing with the SCUD threat of last spring emphasizes how important the relationship is and how well it works when put to the test."

Secretary of State James Baker also traveled to the Middle East and convinced area leaders to join the United States in a special conference in Madrid, Spain. Other countries, eager to participate in the negotiations, were persuaded by President Bush to diplomatically recognize Israel. The Soviet Union, China, India, and Turkey, among others, established relations with Israel either for the first time or renewed official ties broken after the Six-Day War of 1967. The Soviet Union, which voted for the establishment of Israel in 1948 and withdrew recognition in 1967, became a cosponsor, with the United States, of the Madrid Peace Conference.

The Madrid Conference, convened in October 1991, laid the groundwork for serious peace talks involving Israel, Syria, Lebanon, Jordan, and the Palestinians. For the first time, direct face-to-face negotiations with Israel began and met with partial success with the signing of separate peace treaties in 1994 by Israel with Jordan and the Palestinians. Israel's image in the world began to improve.

Meanwhile, in December 1991, at the strong urging of the United States, the United Nations formally rescinded its infamous resolution equating Zionism with racism. Speaking to the General Assembly, President Bush said, "To equate Zionism with the intolerable sin of racism is to twist history. Zionism is not a policy; it was an idea that led to the home of the Jewish people in the State of Israel."

While the peace negotiations began in the Bush administration, the signings took place during the administration of Bill Clinton. Even as many Jewish Americans were preparing to vote against President Bush in the 1992 election, Vice President Quayle spoke to a meeting of AIPAC about the difficulties between Israel and Bush. "The bumps in the road," Quayle said, "trouble him and all of us deeply, but they do not change or threaten the basic principles behind our relationship."

For Jews, Quayle's "bumps" were viewed as boulders. Secretary of State Baker had angered Israelis when he linked American foreign aid to Israel with a demand to end the establishment of Jewish settlements in the West Bank and Gaza. His threat seemed to be part of a pattern in the Bush administration to alternately apply and relax pressure in an effort to force Yitzhak Shamir to the negotiations table.

In March 1992 a charge by the former mayor of New York, Edward Koch, appeared in the *New York Post* against Secretary of State James Baker. Baker, according to Koch, was "criticized recently at a meeting of high-level White House advisers for his belligerent attitude toward Israel." Baker's response to that charge, according to Koch, was "[expletive] the Jews. They don't vote for us anyway!" The secretary strongly denied the report and said he was "deeply offended" by it. But not all Jewish groups in the United States were ready to accept his denial.

President Bush had instituted in 1992 a four-month delay of loan guarantees to Israel to further pressure it to come to the peace negotiations table. When Congress threatened to override his action, he promised a veto. "For the first time in history," Bush said, "the vision of Israelis sitting with their Arab neighbors to talk peace is a real prospect. Nothing should be done that might interfere with this prospect." Israel badly needed the loan guarantees in order to borrow $10 billion from American banks, which was needed to help in the settlement of tens of thousands of new Russian immigrants in Israel. The guarantee would not cost American taxpayers any money—it was merely insurance that Israel would repay the loans. Since its founding in 1948, Israel had never defaulted on a loan. In response to President Bush's statement, Prime Minister Shamir said, "It is inconceivable that our great friend the United States will change its ways and not help Israel."

Concerned about the loan guarantee, one thousand AIPAC members and other supporters of Israel descended upon Capitol Hill on September 12, 1992, to urge Congress to override the president's request to delay the loan guarantee. Angered, President Bush went to the White House pressroom and delivered a stinging statement. "We're up against very strong and effective groups that go up to the Hill. I heard today there were something like a thousand lobbyists on the Hill working the other side of the question. We've got one lonely little guy down here. I think the American people will support me."

American Jews were stunned. The "lobbyists" referred to by the president were ordinary people who were exercising their rights as American citizens to state their views to members of Congress. To many, the president's remarks seemed callous. Indeed, the White House began receiving "congratulatory" letters from anti-Semites. In an attempt to repair the damage, Bush apologized. For American Jews, it was too late. No matter what positive steps he might take, the president could not undo his image.

When it came time for the 1992 U.S. election, Senator Rudy Boschwitz of Minnesota, a Republican and a Jew, tried to repair Bush's image among American Jewish voters. "Is the record perfect?" Boschwitz wrote. "No, but there never has been a presidency with which the Jewish community has not been at odds—never. . . . Would we have preferred a different handling of the loan guarantee issue? Of course. Could we have done without the September news conference? You bet. . . . Everything has to have a bottom line. The pluses and minuses must be weighed, and I believe there can be little question about the outcome of such appraisal fairly made." But Bush received only 11 percent of the Jewish vote, which overwhelmingly went to Bush's Democratic opponent, Governor Bill Clinton of Arkansas. Furthermore, Senator Al Gore of Tennessee, the Democratic nominee for vice president, was a known friend of Israel. He had visited Israel twice and was a leading advocate of a strong U.S.-Israel relationship.

In July 1992, Israeli voters had defeated Yitzhak Shamir's Likud party and brought a coalition government to power led by Yitzhak Rabin of the Labor party. In August, Rabin visited President Bush. "The new government in Israel," Rabin told Bush, "will do its utmost to promote the peacemaking efforts begun and cosponsored by the U.S. under the Madrid framework. . . ." In response, President Bush told reporters, "Prime Minister Rabin has persuaded me that Israel's new government is committed to making these talks succeed. And I call upon the Arab parties to respond in kind. The time has come to make peace, not simply to talk of it."

Between January and August 1993, fourteen secret meetings took place in Oslo, Norway, between Israelis and Palestinians. On August 20 both sides signed a Declaration of Principles. The United States, not a party to the talks, was quickly informed of the historic pact. President Clinton offered his support to both sides.

On September 9 the Norwegian foreign minister delivered a letter to Israeli Foreign Minister Shimon Peres from PLO Chairman Yasir Arafat renouncing terrorism and confirming "the right of the State of Israel to exist in peace and security." In response, Prime Minister Rabin wrote to Arafat that Israel "recognized the PLO as the representative of the Palestinian people and [was ready to] commence negotiations with the PLO within the Middle East peace process." In Washington, President Clinton announced that the United States was resuming a dialogue with the PLO. "For too long," the president said, "the history of the Middle East has been defined in terms of violence and bloodshed.

Today marks the dawning of a new era." The president also announced that the official signing of the Israel-PLO peace agreement would take place in Washington.

On September 13, 1993, Yasir Arafat and Yitzhak Rabin signed the long-awaited peace agreement on the South Lawn of the White House. It was a moment filled with drama. President Clinton awoke at 3:00 A.M. "I just couldn't sleep," he later said. "My mind was so full of the day." Joining the signatories were more than a thousand invited guests, including former American presidents and secretaries of state.

"Enough of blood and tears! Enough!" Rabin told the assembled guests. President Clinton welcomed the guests. "Today," he said, "we bear witness to an extraordinary act in one of history's defining dramas. . . . I pledge the active support of the United States of America to the difficult work that lies ahead. . . ." The ceremony concluded with a scene no one present could have imagined just weeks earlier. With President Clinton in the center, his arms embracing both men, Yitzhak Rabin and Yasir Arafat shook hands. Henry Kissinger called it a "stunning moment." For their historic efforts, Yasir Arafat, Yitzhak Rabin, and Shimon Peres were jointly awarded the 1994 Nobel Peace Prize.

Speaking on September 20 before an audience at Columbia University in New York, Secretary of State Warren Christopher said, "For more than forty-five years, Democratic and Republican administrations have worked tirelessly to break the cycle of violence between Israel and its Arab neighbors. They did so because they understood that the United States has enduring interests in this strategic and historic crossroads; enduring interests in a region where conflict always seems to threaten world peace. . . . The real barrier to peace between the Israelis and the Palestinians—the psychological barrier—has already been breached."

*Another historic event took place on the South Lawn
of the White House on September 13, 1993, with the signing
of a peace agreement between Israel and the Palestine
Liberation Organization (PLO). President Bill Clinton
is flanked by Prime Minister Yitzhak Rabin (left) and
Chairman Yasir Arafat of the PLO.*

Negotiations between both sides on implementation of the agreement soon revealed difficulties as violence by Israeli and Palestinian extremists inflamed the atmosphere. On February 25, 1994, Dr. Baruch Goldstein, an American-born Jewish settler on the West Bank, killed thirty Muslim worshippers at the Tomb of the Patriarchs in Hebron. Several months later, suicide bombers belonging to the Palestinian Hamas group killed a number of Israelis. Both sides, however, had come so far that even these acts of terror could not terminate the peace process. By May 13, 1994, Israel had withdrawn from the Gaza Strip and handed over control of the long-occupied area to Yasir Arafat and the PLO.

On July 25, 1994, Israel signed another peace treaty with a Middle East neighbor, the kingdom of Jordan. Jordan thus joined Egypt to become the second Arab nation to normalize relations with the Jewish state. Again, the American president's role was pivotal. Bill Clinton traveled to Israel to stand beside Rabin and Jordan's King Hussein as they signed the formal treaty. The next day the president spoke in the Knesset. "In times of war and times of peace," Clinton said, "every President of the United States since Harry Truman, and every Congress, has understood the importance of Israel. The survival of Israel is important not only to our interests, but to every single value we hold dear as a people. . . ."

The president told the lawmakers that the United States was committed to helping Israel economically and diplomatically. Clinton promised to maintain a $3 billion annual aid level for Israel as well as support for security aid and development. In closing, Clinton said, "Your journey is our journey, and America will stand with you, now and always."

Upon receiving an award from Prime Minister Rabin on behalf of the United Jewish Appeal in October 1995, President Bill Clinton talked about his role in the Middle East peace process. "We have tried to be a full and reliable partner. I am proud of the agreements that we have worked hard to bring about. I am proud of the handshakes that sealed them—handshakes I never thought I would live to see." As his audience laughed, the president turned to Yitzhak Rabin and said, "I'm not sure he did either." No one in the room could know that within a few weeks, Prime Minister Yitzhak Rabin would be dead—killed by an assassin's bullet.

FRIENDS AND ALLIES

Shalom, haver.

—President Bill Clinton

At 9:40 P.M. on Saturday, November 4, 1995, Israel's prime minister, Yitzhak Rabin, escorted by security officials, prepared to enter his armored limousine. Before police could react, a slightly built young man quickly approached from the rear and fired two shots at point-blank range. Almost instantly, the prime minister of Israel lay dead on the street. The crime was even more traumatic to Israelis when they learned that the assassin was not an Arab terrorist but a twenty-five-year-old Jewish law student. Just moments earlier, the prime minister had spoken to a massive peace rally of 100,000 people in the heart of Tel Aviv.

Israel was a divided nation. Some Israelis, mainly religious Jews and settlers in Gaza and the West Bank, felt that Rabin had gone too far in his negotiations with the Palestinians. They did not want Israel to surrender occupied territory for a peace in which they had little confidence. They did not trust Yasir Arafat and the PLO to honor any agreements with Israel. On the other side were the Israelis represented by the massive outpouring that night in Tel Aviv, who strongly believed that a negotiated settlement, including the return of land, offered the best solution to the continuing state of war with the Palestinians.

"I have always believed," Rabin told the crowd, "most of the nation wants peace and is prepared to take risks for peace. And you here, who have come to take a stand for peace, as well as many others who are not here, are proof that the nation truly wants peace and rejects violence. Violence is undermining the foundations of Israeli democracy. It must be rejected and condemned and it must be contained. It is not the way of the State of Israel. Democracy is our way." Then, in a profoundly prophetic statement, Rabin told the crowd, "There are enemies of the peace process, and they try to hurt us."

President Clinton was deeply shocked at the news of Rabin's death. Speaking directly from the White House Rose Garden to the people of Israel, the president said, "I want you to know that the hearts and prayers of all Americans are with you. Just as America has stood by you in moments of crisis and triumph so now we all stand by you in this moment of grieving and loss." The president tearfully concluded, "Yitzhak Rabin was my partner and my friend. I admired him, and I loved him very much. Because words cannot express my true feelings, let me just say *shalom, haver*—good-bye, friend." In the days that followed, the phrase "shalom, haver" appeared on homemade signs and bumper stickers throughout Israel as a symbol of the close relationship between the United States and Israel. In both countries the assassination of Rabin was compared to the earlier untimely deaths of President John F. Kennedy, assassinated in 1963, and his brother, Senator Robert Kennedy, killed in 1968.

It has become customary for the vice president of the United States to represent the nation at important foreign funerals. But, on November 5, 1995, the vice president stayed in Washington while the remaining leadership of

Most Israelis were determined that the assassination of Prime Minister Rabin in 1995 would not deter the peace process he had worked hard to initiate. It was because of this process, in fact, that a young Israeli law student, disgruntled at Rabin's negotiations with the PLO, carried out the murder of the prime minister. These three teenagers set up a memorial outside the Israeli parliament soon after learning of Rabin's death.

the United States government traveled to Israel for the funeral of Yitzhak Rabin. Accompanying President Bill Clinton were his wife, Hillary, Secretary of State Warren Christopher, Speaker of the House Newt Gingrich, and Senate Majority Leader Robert Dole. Forty members of Congress also attended, as did former presidents Jimmy Carter and George Bush and former secretaries of state Cyrus Vance and George Shultz. The president explained that the large American delegation was to show "that the United States still stands as a genuine friend and partner to the people of Israel, Republicans and Democrats alike."

At the funeral service, the president eulogized, "Your prime minister was a martyr for peace, but he was a victim of hate. Surely, we must learn from his martyrdom that if people cannot let go of the hatred of their enemies, they risk sowing the seeds of hatred among themselves." Then, referring to America's experience, he added, "On behalf of my nation that knows its own long litany of loss from Abraham Lincoln, to President Kennedy, to Martin Luther King, do not let that happen to you." In a poignant act, Senator Edward M. Kennedy sprinkled earth on Rabin's grave that he had brought with him from the Arlington National Cemetery graves of John and Robert Kennedy.

A few weeks later Rabin's successor as prime minister, Shimon Peres, traveled to Washington. At the White House, President Clinton said, "I want to welcome the prime minister here. It's a pleasure to have him here and a privilege to continue our partnership, our search for peace." Peres responded, "May I say the president has changed our hearts and changed our language. He's changed our hearts by a very moving appearance at the funeral of the late Yitzhak Rabin. And he changed our language by adding two words that were never in our vocabulary: 'Shalom, haver.' It has become a household expression."

Within a few months Israel was wracked by a series of suicide bombings by Palestinian terrorists, which claimed the lives of sixty people, including several Americans. Hundreds were wounded. Nervous Israelis questioned the value of any peace agreements with Palestinians. Since signing the Declaration of Principles between Israel and the PLO in September 1993, nearly two hundred people, including five Americans, had been killed by acts of terror committed by Palestinians.

To calm the fears of Israelis and assure the shaky peace process, President Clinton videotaped a message, which was broadcast to the people of Israel. "I share your determination to do everything possible to bring this horror to an end," he said, "and to bring those responsible to justice. Our nations both cherish the same ideals: freedom, tolerance, and democracy. And we know that whenever these ideals are under siege in one country they are threatened everywhere." On September 28, 1995, the United States Senate passed a resolution condemning the terror.

The president convened an unprecedented summit meeting on terrorism at the Egyptian resort of Sharm al-Sheikh, attended by leaders of the European Community, Russia, Canada, the United States, and thirteen Arab nations. At the conclusion of the summit meeting, on March 14, 1996, during his third visit to Israel in less than two years, President Clinton pledged $100 million in aid to fight terrorism and assured Israelis that "the Middle East is changing. We must not—we will not—let terror reverse history."

During his whirlwind trip to Israel, Clinton visited the grave of Yitzhak Rabin. Following a Jewish custom, he placed a stone on Rabin's tombstone—a stone from the spot on the White House lawn where Rabin had shaken hands with Yasir Arafat. At a press conference, President Clinton said, "Just as America walks with you every step of the way as you work toward peace, we stand with you now in defending all that you are and all that has been accomplished." Speaking of the president's visit, Prime Minister

Peres told a radio audience, "Everything he does points to an extraordinary friendship. . . . It really touches the heart."

Speaking at a press conference the following day in Israel, Clinton said, "I came here more than anything else just to once again express the solidarity of the United States with Israel, grief at your loss, and our determination to do what we can both to restore your security and to preserve the march of peace." He didn't mention it to the press, but the president also was in Israel to indirectly support the election campaign of Prime Minister Rabin's successor, Shimon Peres.

President Clinton was anxious to keep the peace process alive, but he was also realistic about the events in the Middle East. "The conflict of decades," he told an AIPAC convention in 1995, "will not end with the stroke of a pen or even two pens, but consider how far we have come. No one who was there will ever forget that brilliant day on the White House lawn when Prime Minister Rabin and Chairman Arafat resolved to end their conflict. No one who was there will ever forget the Patriarchs' Walk when Israel and Jordan made peace after sixteen years. Those were two of my proudest moments as President. They should be two of every American's proudest moments for our country in the last two years."

On April 30, 1996, a month after President Clinton's visit to Israel, Prime Minister Peres was in Washington to join Clinton in signing the U.S.-Israel Counter-terrorism Cooperation Accord. The agreement allocated the nearly $100 million Clinton had pledged for research, development, training, and investigation to combat terrorism. In response to a reporter's question about the upcoming elections in Israel, President Clinton responded, "Israel and the United States are friends and allies, and will be—no matter who is elected." Then, thinking of the upcoming presidential election in the U.S., the president said, "I hope that will also be the case no matter who is elected in November in the United States. Our policy on that has not changed and will not and should not."

When the Israeli elections were over at the end of May, President Clinton's preferred candidate, Shimon Peres, had been replaced by the American-educated Likud leader Benjamin Netanyahu. Peres was an architect of the peace process; Netanyahu viewed the quick pace of the process with alarm. He feared that Israel was giving up too much too fast without any ironclad guarantees from the Arabs that terrorism would cease. Although surprised and disappointed at the turn of events, the president telephoned his congratulations and invited Netanyahu to Washington. The president later said, "The historic relationship between the United States and Israel has not and will not change."[1]

In July 1996, Netanyahu, as his predecessors had done, made the expected official trip to Washington. In many ways the new prime minister understood America better than Rabin and Peres. He spoke fluent English, had grown up attending American schools, and served as a diplomat in New York and Washington. Speaking before a joint session of Congress, Netanyahu glowingly described his respect and appreciation for America's continual support of Israel. "You, the people of America, offered the fledgling Jewish state succor and support. You stood by us time and time again, against the forces of tyranny and totalitarianism. I know that I speak for every Israeli and every Jew throughout the world when I say to you today: Thank you, people of America."

Support for Israel by the United States has been constant since 1948 even with frequent disagreements on strategies and policies. The support has continued despite changing political leadership in both democracies. In Israel the Labor party rule of Ben-Gurion, Meir, Rabin, and Peres alternated with the Likud leadership of Begin, Shamir, and

Netanyahu. In the United States, Democratic and Republican presidents and members of Congress have offered continual basic support.

But the family-like relations have often yielded family-like squabbles. As in most families, there have been ups and downs. Jewish settlement in the West Bank and Gaza, for example, resulted in opposition from the Nixon White House, which called them "illegal," and from President Clinton, who called them "obstacles to peace." In spite of the spats, the underlying commitments remained strong. The 1981 Memorandum of Understanding led to arrangements in a number of special military and civilian fields. In the 1980s the United States recognized Israel as a "strategic asset" and a "major non-NATO ally," joining such nations as Britain, France, and Germany.

What makes the relationship between the United States and Israel so unique? The ties are deeply rooted in the cultures of both nations. Perhaps Prime Minister Peres put it best in his 1996 address before Congress: "For us, the United States of America is a commitment to values before an expression of might. For us, the vast discovery of America is its Constitution even more than its continent—the Constitution enriched by its biblical foundation." Peres then recalled the historical ties between the United States and the Holy Land. "From our school days we remembered the proposal of John Adams that the imagery of ancient Israel captivated the Constitutional Congress in 1776. We recalled Benjamin Franklin's idea to incorporate into the Great Seal of the new Confederation the image of Moses raising his staff dividing the Red Sea. We remembered Thomas Jefferson suggesting that the image of the children of Israel struggling through the wilderness, led by a pillar of cloud by day, by a pillar of fire by night—that this image be the symbol of the young republic, to become the great republic."

According to two former Israeli prime ministers, AIPAC has been the "spearhead of the special relations between

Washington and Jerusalem" and "the strongest bridge between the American people and the State of Israel." Whenever there is legislation in Congress relating to Israel, AIPAC is able to mobilize its network of supporters to contact lawmakers in Washington. Thomas Dine, AIPAC's former executive director, said, "Issues are won or lost on Capitol Hill not because of what takes place in Washington, but because of what constituents want."

Not always successful in its efforts, AIPAC is still a widely respected model for other citizens' advocacy groups in Washington. Its actions do not differ from those of other ethnic, business, and special-interest groups. Each seeks to influence government policy. One member of Congress said of AIPAC, "They bring clarity of purpose with passionate commitment to everything they do. They are never ambiguous. The president's foreign policy should be so effective." President Clinton credited AIPAC with "helping to make the partnership between the United States and Israel what it is today."

Some in Washington have other views of AIPAC. Although it is forbidden by law from accepting and distributing political money, individual AIPAC members are free to contribute to any political campaign. They naturally gravitate toward those candidates with proven records of support for Israel. "No one can run for national office without Jewish support," charged one disgruntled political fundraiser. Thomas Dine once said that candidates "know that we can put them in touch with people in their areas who want to hear their views on Israel and who can help them."

Since its birth in 1948, Israel has been the only true democracy in the Middle East, one of the most volatile parts of the world. The peace process could never have begun unless Israel felt the confidence to take risks. That security came from the economic and diplomatic support of the United States. At international forums, including the United Nations, the United States was often Israel's sole supporter against the strident voices of the Soviet Union and Arab and Third World nations. "If Israel is ever forced to walk out of the UN," President Reagan once said, "the United States and Israel will walk out together." For many years since the 1970s, Israel has been the largest recipient of American military and economic aid. Beginning in the Reagan administration, much of this aid was given to Israel in the form of outright grants. Over the years, free-trade agreements, research programs, joint military exercises, and the sharing of intelligence have benefited both countries.

The signing of formal peace treaties with Egypt, Jordan, and the Palestinians, coupled with the end of the Cold War, brought Israel out of its diplomatic isolation. The influx of large numbers of highly educated Jews from the former Soviet Union greatly increased Israel's standing in the computer and engineering fields. Israel in the 1990s had more scientists and engineers per capita than any other country (including three times as many as the United States). Prime Minister Netanyahu alluded to the effect that the new prosperity brought to Israel. "With America's help," he assured Congress, "Israel has grown to be a powerful modern state. I believe that it has matured enough to begin approaching a state of self-reliance. . . . I believe there can be no greater tribute to America's long-standing economic aid to Israel than for us to be able to say: We are going to achieve economic independence."

Israeli manufacturers of high-tech electronics, medical equipment, drugs, and a wide array of military equipment do much of their business outside of Israel. In 1995, Israel became New York State's sixth-largest international trading partner. Israeli firms have begun to establish themselves in the United States. Scitex digital color image equipment is used by major newspapers and magazines; drugs developed by Teva and Interpharm help American doctors treat a variety of illnesses from pinkeye to multiple sclerosis.

American companies have also discovered the rich pool of talent in Israel. Firms such as Motorola, Sara Lee, Revlon, Intel, and Hewlett Packard have established plants in Israel. One manager explained that Motorola established itself in Israel because "we needed the knowledge that Israel offers in architecture and algorithm development, science, and math." To help facilitate this international activity, the Israel-America Chamber of Commerce and Industry was founded to advance "commercial and economic relations between the United States and Israel."

One result of Israel's economic development has been less reliance on the financial support of the American Jewish community. Local Jewish federations have begun to redirect a larger proportion of their funding from Israel to needed social services at home. Boston's Combined Jewish Philanthropies' overseas funding dropped from $12.9 million in 1990 to $7 million in 1995.

The American fascination with Israel is equaled only by the Israeli fascination with America. Visitors to Israel's largest cities feel right at home when they see signs in Hebrew and English. American fast-food restaurants such as McDonald's, Pizza Hut, and Burger King are sprouting throughout the country, as are branches of American stores such as Ace Hardware, Timberland, Toys R Us, and Office Depot. American-style malls and supermarkets are quickly replacing small "mom and pop" stores. American songs, films, and television programs are wildly popular.

In the 1996 Israeli elections, American-style campaigning predominated. The bumper stickers, slick television commercials, and thirty-second sound-bytes were avidly adopted by the major candidates. The successful candidate for prime minister, Benjamin Netanyahu, even hired an American campaign strategist, Arthur Finkelstein, to direct his successful bid for election.

Frequent airline service links both countries. Tourism is one of Israel's major industries. Jewish and Christian groups from the United States come to visit the religious sites. Individuals come as volunteers or to study at Israel's prestigious universities and religious schools. A number of Christian Zionist groups exist in the United States, mainly allied with the political and religious right. Their religious objectives are to "show concern for the Jewish people and the reborn State of Israel by taking part in preparing the way of the Lord and anticipating His reign from Jerusalem."

One organization, Voices United for Israel, links more than 150 churches, synagogues, and organizations dedicated to a "safe and secure Israel." Their annual convention has been addressed by leaders of Congress and Middle East experts. The organization issued a resolution, which called "on the Congress of the United States to maintain and enhance Israel's economic stability through foreign aid commitments . . . thus promoting the interests of the United States in the region."

Israel frequently sponsors "fact-finding" trips to Israel for American politicians. One member of Congress, Matt Salmon of Arizona, wrote that the goal of his 1995 trip was "to gain insights on U.S.-Israel relations, the peace talks, security, and the status of economic and political trends." Like many visitors, he had a second and more personal goal: "to enhance my study of scripture by seeing the places so vividly described in the Bible."

Congressman Salmon met with Israeli government officials, visited the Yad Vashem Holocaust Memorial, the Golan Heights, the Western Wall, and Bethlehem. "Walking where the prophets walked," he later wrote, "going to the places that exist at the spiritual epicenter of the world, and meeting the people who live among so much history brought the Bible more vividly to life for me than ever before. . . . I came away with my faith reinvigorated, and with my confidence bolstered that Israel is vital to stability in the Middle East."

In turn, visits to America by Israeli teen groups have proven to be popular and helpful in getting Israel's message across to young people in the United States. One organization, the America-Israel Friendship League, brings more than one hundred Israeli students to the United States and fifty American students to Israel to talk to school groups and stay with local families. One Israeli teen told an audience, "Every year, Israel is becoming more like America, but we're still different." Other students credited their viewing of American television shows in Israel with making them feel at home in the United States.

"The United States and Israel have a special relationship," said former Secretary of State Warren Christopher. "The bonds between us, our shared democratic values, our belief in the rule of law, our commitment to peace . . . those bonds are enduring and unshakable. They will remain as strong in the future as they have been in the past."

TIMELINE

70	Destruction of the Second Temple in Jerusalem
1881	First Aliya—Jewish settlers from Russia arrive in Palestine
1897	First Zionist Congress
1903	Second Aliya
1904	Death of Theodor Herzl, founder of political Zionism
1917	The Balfour Declaration
1919	Third Aliya
1920	British mandate over Palestine begins
1924	Fourth Aliya
1929	Fifth Aliya
1939–1945	World War II and the Holocaust
1945	Aliya Bet—illegal immigration of Jews to Palestine
1947	United Nations partition plan for Palestine
1948	Proclamation of the State of Israel David Ben-Gurion becomes Israel's first prime minister Recognition by the United States Attack by five neighboring Arab nations and the ensuing War of Independence

1949 Israel admitted to the United Nations
      Armistice agreements
      Tripartite Agreement (United States, Britain, France)

1950 Jewish "lobby" established in the United States
      Border tensions with neighboring Arab countries

1956 Sinai war

1957 Israel withdraws from Sinai
      UN observers stationed on Egyptian border

1962 First direct sale of weapons to Israel by the United States

1964 Founding of the Palestine Liberation Organization (PLO)

1967 Six-Day War
      UN Resolution 242

1969 War of attrition begins

1973 Yom Kippur War
      UN Resolution 338
      Geneva Conference

1974 President Richard Nixon visits Israel

1975 UN vote declares "Zionism is racism"

1976 President Jimmy Carter endorses a Palestinian state

1977 Anwar Sadat visits Israel

1978 Camp David talks
      Nobel Peace Prize awarded to Sadat and Menachem Begin

1979 Peace treaty signed in Washington between Israel and Egypt
      President Carter visits Israel

1981 Memorandum of Understanding between Israel and the
      United States
      President Sadat assassinated

1982 Israel invades Lebanon
      Sabra and Shatila camp massacres

1987 Intifada begins

1988 Jordan renounces claims to West Bank

Yasir Arafat announces acceptance of UN Resolutions 242 and 338 and renounces terrorism
Palestinian State proclaimed at Algiers conference

1991   Gulf War: SCUD missiles fall on Israel
UN repeals "Zionism is racism" vote
Soviet Union reestablishes relations with Israel
Madrid Peace Conference organized by the United States

1992   Yitzhak Rabin becomes Israel's prime minister

1993   Secret meetings between representatives of Israel and the PLO in Oslo, Norway
Arafat and Rabin sign letters of mutual recognition

1994   King Hussein of Jordan and Prime Minister Rabin of Israel sign peace treaty

1995   Prime Minister Rabin assassinated

1996   Benjamin Netanyahu elected prime minister

NOTES

Chapter One

1. Raphael Patai, ed., and Harry Zohn, trans., *Complete Diaries of Theodor Herzl* (New York: Herzl Press, 1960), p. 581.
2. Quoted in Melvin Urofsky, *A Voice That Spoke for Justice* (Albany: State University of New York, 1982), p. 23.
3. Ibid. p. 25.
4. Edward Tivnan, *The Lobby: Jewish Political Power and American Foreign Policy* (New York: Simon & Schuster, 1987), p. 17.
5. Quoted in Robert Silverberg, *If I Forget Thee, O Jerusalem* (New York: Morrow, 1970), p. 89.
6. Quoted in *A Voice That Spoke for Justice*, p. 148.
7. Ibid. p. 240.
8. Quoted in Jack R. Fischel, "Rabbis and Leaders—Silver and Wise" in *American Zionist*, Volume LXXII, April/May 1983, p. 6.
9. Quoted in Walter Laquer, *A History of Zionism* (New York: Holt, Rinehart and Winston, 1972), p. 566.

Chapter Two

1. Quoted in Michael Cohen, *Truman and Israel* (Berkeley: University of California Press, 1990), p. 167.
2. Letter from Eddie Jacobson to Harry Truman, October 3, 1947, from the Harry Truman Library.
3. Quoted in *Truman and Israel*, p. 186.
4. Quoted in Margaret Truman, *Harry S. Truman* (New York: Quill, 1972), p. 388.

5. Quoted in Zvi Ganin, *Truman, American Jewry, and Israel* (New York: Holmes and Meier, 1979), p. 168.

Chapter Three
1. *The Washington Post*, May 14, 1948.
2. Telegram from Harry Truman to David Ben-Gurion, from the Harry Truman Library.
3. Speech by John F. Kennedy, February 24, 1952, from the John F. Kennedy Library.
4. Quoted in Peter Kihss, "Truman Links U.S. to Mideast Peace," *The New York Times*, January 13, 1958, p. 20.
5. Quoted in Winocoor, *American Zionist*, p. 7.
6. Ibid. p. 9.
7. David Ben-Gurion, *Israel: Years of Challenge* (New York: Holt, Rinehart and Winston, 1963), p. 87.
8. Quoted in *American Zionist*, February 15, 1954, p. 20.
9. American Jewish Committee, *Report From Israel*, April 1954.
10. *Israel: Years of Challenge*, p. 72.
11. Stephen Ambrose, *Eisenhower* (New York: Simon & Schuster, 1984), p. 315.
12. *Israel: Years of Challenge*, p. 70.
13. Quoted in Herbert Druks, *The U.S. and Israel 1945–1973* (New York: Speller, 1979), p. 61.
14. Ibid. p. 57.
15. David Ben-Gurion, *Israel: A Personal History* (New York: Funk and Wagnalls, 1949), pp. 474-476.
16. Quoted in *The U.S. and Israel 1945–1973*, p. 56.
17. Ibid. p. 61.
18. American Jewish Committee, *Report From Israel*, March 1956.
19. Isaac Alteras, "Eisenhower, American Jewry, and Israel," *American Jewish Archives*, Volume XXXVII, November 1985, p. 267.
20. *The U.S. and Israel 1945–1973*, p. 66.
21. "Eisenhower, American Jewry, and Israel," p. 264.
22. Ibid. p. 272.

Chapter Four
1. Speech by John F. Kennedy, February 4, 1952, from the John F. Kennedy Library.
2. David Ben-Gurion Oral History, July 16, 1965, from the John F. Kennedy Library.

3. Quoted in Dan Raviv and Yossi Melman, *Friends in Deed* (New York: Hyperion, 1994), pp. 103–104.

4. Report, Central Intelligence Agency, January 18, 1961, from the John F. Kennedy Library.

5. David Ben-Gurion Oral History.

6. Telegram from John F. Kennedy to Levi Eshkol, October 2, 1962, from the John F. Kennedy Library.

7. Memorandum of Conversation of John F. Kennedy and Foreign Minister Meir, December 27, 1962, from the John F. Kennedy Library.

8. Ibid.

9. Quoted in David Schoenbaum, *The United States and the State of Israel* (New York: Oxford University Press, 1993), p. 137.

10. Golda Meir, *My Life* (New York: Putnam, 1975), p. 313.

11. Quoted in Norman Finkelstein, *With Heroic Truth: The Life of Edward R. Murrow* (New York: Clarion, 1997), p. 128.

12. *U.S. News*, April 17, 1967, p. 176.

13. Myer Feldman Oral History, August 26, 1967, from the John F. Kennedy Library.

14. Quoted in Yaacov Bar-Siman-Tov, *Israel, the Superpowers, and War in the Middle East* (New York: Praeger, 1987), p. 116.

15. Herbert Druks, *The U.S. and Israel 1946–1973* (New York: Speller, 1979), p. 76.

16. Quoted in Robert St. John, *Ben-Gurion* (Garden City, NY: Doubleday, 1959), p. 439.

17. John P. Roche Oral History, July 16, 1970, from the Lyndon Baines Johnson Library, p. 68.

18. Quoted in Melvin Urofsky, *We Are One!* (Garden City, NY: Doubleday, 1978), p. 349.

19. Quoted in *Israel, the Superpowers, and War in the Middle East*, p. 123.

Chapter Five

1. Abba Eban, *Personal Witness: Israel Through My Eyes* (New York: Putnam, 1992), p. 202.

2. Quoted in Melvin Urofsky, *We Are One!* (Garden City, NY: Doubleday, 1978), p. 388.

3. Quoted in *The New York Times*, December 27, 1970.

4. Quoted in Yaacov Bar-Siman-Tov, *Israel, the Superpowers, and the War in the Middle East* (New York: Praeger, 1987), p. 189.

5. Golda Meir, *My Life* (New York: Putnam, 1975), p. 431.

6. Ibid.
7. Quoted in Herbert Druks, *The U.S. and Israel 1945–1973* (New York: Speller, 1979), p. 112.
8. Quoted in Stephen E. Ambrose, *Nixon: Ruin and Recovery 1973–1990* (New York: Simon & Schuster, 1991), p. 246.
9. Henry Kissinger, *Years of Upheaval* (Boston: Little, Brown, 1982), pp. 542-543.
10. *My Life*, p. 441.
11. Quoted in Walter Isaacson, *Kissinger* (New York: Simon & Schuster, 1992), p. 536.
12. Memorandum from Henry Kissinger to Gerald R. Ford, September 10, 1974, from the Gerald R. Ford Library, Ann Arbor, Michigan.
13. Quoted in Peter Golden, *Quiet Diplomat, Max Fisher* (New York: Cornwall Press, 1992), p. 333.
14. Notes of Meeting between President Gerald Ford and Max Fisher, the White House, April 9, 1975, from the Gerald R. Ford Library, Ann Arbor, Michigan.
15. White House Memorandum, February 8, 1975, from the Gerald R. Ford Library, Ann Arbor, Michigan.
16. State Department telegram from the American ambassador in Israel to the secretary of state, February 7, 1975, from the Gerald R. Ford Library, Ann Arbor, Michigan.
17. White House Memorandum of Conversation, June 26, 1975, from the Gerald R. Ford Library, Ann Arbor, Michigan.
18. White House Memorandum, June 13, 1975, from the Gerald R. Ford Library, Ann Arbor, Michigan.
19. Memorandum from Robert Goldwyn to Donald Rumsfeld, May 1, 1975, from the Gerald R. Ford Library, Ann Arbor, Michigan.

Chapter Six
1. *The New York Times*, August 9, 1978, p. 53.
2. Jimmy Carter, *Talking Peace* (New York: Dutton, 1993), p. 15.
3. Quoted in Dan Raviv and Yossi Melman, *Friends in Deed* (New York: Hyperion, 1994), p. 194.
4. *The New York Times*, May 22, 1981.
5. Quoted in *Friends in Deed*, p. 214.

BIBLIOGRAPHY

Abodaher, David. *Youth in the Middle East*. New York: Franklin Watts, 1990.

Ambros, Stephen. *Nixon: Ruin and Recovery 1973–1990*. New York: Touchstone Books, 1991.

Bar-Siman-Tov, Yaacov. *Israel, the Superpowers, and the War in the Middle East*. New York: Praeger, 1987.

Ben-Gurion, David. *Israel: Years of Challenge*. New York: Holt, Rinehart and Winston, 1963.

Ben-Zvi, Abraham. *The United States and Israel*. New York: Columbia University Press, 1993.

Blitzer, Wolf. *Territory of Lies*. New York: Harper and Row, 1989.

Cannon, Lou. *President Reagan: The Role of a Lifetime*. New York: Simon & Schuster, 1991.

Carter, Jimmy. *Talking Peace*. New York: Dutton, 1993.

Cockburn, Andrew, and Leslie Cockburn. *Dangerous Liaison: The Inside Story of the U.S.-Israeli Covert Relationship*. New York: Harper and Row, 1991.

Cohen, Michael J. *Truman and Israel*. Berkeley: University of California Press, 1990.

Davis, Moshe, ed. *The Yom Kippur War, Israel, and the Jewish People*. New York: Arno Press, 1974.

Druks, Herbert. *The U.S. and Israel 1945–1973*. New York: Speller, 1979.

Eban, Abba. *Voice of Israel*. New York: Horizon Press, 1957.

Ganin, Zvi. *Truman, American Jewry, and Israel 1945–1948*. New York: Holmes and Meier, 1979.

Goldberg, J. J. *Jewish Power*. Reading, MA: Addison-Wesley, 1996.

Golden, Peter. *Quiet Diplomat, Max M. Fisher*. New York: Cornwall Press, 1992.

Grose, Peter. *Israel in the Mind of America*. New York: Knopf, 1984.

Herzog, Chaim. *The Arab-Israeli Wars*. New York: Vintage Books, 1984.

Isaacson, Walter. *Kissinger*. New York: Simon & Schuster, 1992.

Klieman, Aaron. *Israel and the World After 40 Years*. Washington: Pergamon-Brassey's International Defense Publishers, 1990.

Kort, Michael. *Yitzhak Rabin*. Brookfield, CT: Millbrook, 1996.

Lebeson, Anita Libman. *Pilgrim People*. New York: Harper, 1950.

McCullough, David. *Truman*. New York: Simon & Schuster, 1992.

Meir, Golda. *My Life*. New York: G. P. Putnam's Sons, 1975.

Raviv, Dan, and Yossi Melman. *Every Spy a Prince*. Boston: Houghton-Mifflin, 1990.

Raviv, Dan, and Yossi Melman. *Friends in Deed: Inside the U.S.-Israel Alliance*. New York: Hyperion, 1994.

Rose, Norman. *Chaim Weizmann*. New York: Viking, 1986.

Safran, Nadav. *Israel: The Embattled Ally*. Cambridge, MA: Harvard University Press, 1978.

St. John, Robert. *Ben-Gurion*. Garden City, NY: Doubleday, 1959.

St. John, Robert. *Eban*. New York: Dell, 1972.

Schoenbaum, David. *The United States and the State of Israel*. New York: Oxford University Press, 1993.

Silver, Eric. *Begin, the Haunted Prophet*. New York: Random House, 1984.

Silverberg, Robert. *If I Forget Thee, O Jerusalem*. New York: Morrow, 1970.

Snetsinger, John. *Truman, the Jewish Vote, and the Creation of Israel*. Stanford, CA: Hoover Institution, 1974.

Tivnan, Edward. *Lobby: Jewish Political Power and American Foreign Policy*. New York: Simon & Schuster, 1987.

Truman, Margaret. *Harry S. Truman*. New York: Morrow, 1973.

Urofsky, Melvin I. *American Zionism From Herzl to the Holocaust*. Garden City, NY: Doubleday, 1975.

Urofsky, Melvin I. *We Are One!* Garden City, NY: Doubleday, 1978.

Weizman, Ezer. *The Battle for Peace*. New York: Bantam, 1981.

INDEX

Kennedy, Edward M., 150
Kennedy, John F., 50, *51*, 52, 68-
	71, *72*, 84, 148, 150
Kennedy, Robert F., 148, 150
Kennedy, Thomas, 14
Khartoum Conference (1967),
	83
Khrushchev, Nikita, 60
Kiryat Shimona, 101
Kishinev massacre, 20, 28
Kissinger, Henry, 90, 92, 94-
	100, 102, 103, 105, 107, *108*,
	109, 118, 144
Klinghoffer, Leon, 131
Koch, Edward, 141
Kosygin, Aleksei, 82, 97
Kuwait, 77, 136

Labor party, 114, 153
Lansing, Robert, 26
League of Nations, 27, 29
League of Women Voters, 110
Lebanon, 46, 87, 118, 127-128,
	140
Lewis, Samuel, 126
Likud party, 114, 115, 135, 153
Lodge, Henry Cabot, Jr., 55, 62

Mack, Julian W., 23
Madrid Peace Conference
	(1991), 140
Marcus, Mickey, 65
Marshall, Louis, 22
Meir, Golda, 46, 65, 67, 70-71,
	72, 84-86, 88, *89*, 90-92, 95-
	97, 99, 100, 117, 153
Memorandum of Understand-
	ing (1981), 124-126, 154
Mendelssohn, Moses, 11
Miller, Israel, 103

Mitla Pass, 109
Monotheism, 11
Moshav Yahud, 52
Mossad, 129
Moynihan, Daniel P., 110
Mubarak, Hosni, 123
Munich Olympics (1972), 86,
	91
Murrow, Edward R., 73

Nasser, Gamal Abdel, 57-58,
	59, 60-62, 65, 66, 74-76, 78,
	81, 87-88, 91, 113
National Community Rela-
	tions Advisory Council, 49
Nazi Germany, 29, 30, 35
Negev Desert, 38, 42, 53, 58
Netanyahu, Benjamin, 112,
	153, 154, 156, 157
Netanyahu, Yonatan, 111-112
Nixon, Richard M., 68, 85, 88,
	89, 90-92, 94-101, 105, 111
Noah, Mordecai Manuel, 14-15
Nuclear weapons, 67, 69, 96,
	125, 138-139

Oil, 40, 57, 98, 110, 121, 136
Osirak nuclear reactor, 125,
	126, 137, 138

Pakistan, 57
Palestine, 19, 20, 22, 26-32, 35,
	36, 38-43, 45
Palestine Liberation Organiza-
	tion (PLO), 86-87, 115, 127,
	128, 130, 131, 134, 135, 143,
	146, 147
Palestinians, 47, 48, 114-115,
	126-129, 133-135, 140, 143-
	147, 150, 156

ABOUT THE AUTHOR

Norman H. Finkelstein is the author of several books for young adults, including *Remember Not to Forget: A Memory of the Holocaust* and *With Heroic Truth: The Life of Edward R. Murrow*. He is a librarian at the Edward Devotion School of the Brookline, Massachusetts, public schools, and has been active at Hebrew College as an instructor and as educational director at Camp Yavneh, the college's summer school and camp. Educated at Hebrew College and Boston University, he lives with his wife in Framingham, Massachusetts.